SPECIAL SERIES No. 34   1 AUGUST 1945

JAPANESE TANK AND ANTITANK WARFARE

MILITARY INTELLIGENCE DIVISION
WAR DEPARTMENT · WASHINGTON DC

Published by Books Express Publishing
Copyright © Books Express, 2011
ISBN 978-1-780390-71-0

Books Express publications are available from all good retail and online booksellers. For publishing proposals and direct ordering please contact us at: info@books-express.com

SPECIAL SERIES NO. 34   *1 AUGUST 1945*

JAPANESE TANK AND ANTITANK WARFARE

MILITARY INTELLIGENCE DIVISION
WAR DEPARTMENT • *WASHINGTON, D. C.*

MILITARY INTELLIGENCE
SERVICE
WAR DEPARTMENT
WASHINGTON 25, D. C.

SPECIAL SERIES
No. 34
MID 461

Notice

This issue of SPECIAL SERIES supersedes SPECIAL SERIES No. 26, *Japanese Tanks and Tank Tactics*. It also replaces the tentative edition of *Japanese Tank and Antitank Warfare* published 25 June 1945. It is based on reasonably confirmed information from authoritative sources up to 15 July 1945.

Reproduction within the military service is encouraged provided that the source is stated, the classification is maintained, and one copy of the publication in which the material is reproduced is forwarded to the Military Intelligence Service War Department, Washington 25, D. C.

DISTRIBUTION:

Refer to FM 21-6 for explanation of distribution formula.

Cover Illustration

The illustration on the cover shows the rear of a Type 94 (1934) medium tank with ditching tail.

CONTENTS

	Page
CHAPTER I. JAPANESE ARMORED FIGHTING VEHICLES	1
Introduction	1
Tankettes	3
Type 92 (1932) Tankette	3
Type 94 (1934) Tankette	6
Type 97 (1937) Tankette	8
Light Tanks	15
Type 93 (1933) Light Tank	15
Type 93 (1933) Light Tank (Improved Version)	18
Type 95 (1935) Light Tank	18
Type 98 (1938) Light Tank	33
"Keni" Light Tank	34
Medium Tanks	34
Type 89A (1929) Medium Tank	34
Type 89B (1929) Medium Tank	37
Type 94 (1934) Medium Tank	38
Type 97 (1937) Medium Tank	43
Type 97 (1937) Medium Tank (Improved Version)	50
Amphibious Tank	54
Flame-Throwing Tanks	63
Flame-Throwing Tanks on Luzon	63
Self-Propelled Guns	67
Self-Propelled 15-cm Howitzer	67
Type 2 (1942) 75-mm Self-Propelled Gun	70
105-mm Self-Propelled Weapons	72
Armored Cars	73
Type 92 (1932) Navy Armored Car	73
Type 93 (1933) "Sumida" Armored Car	74
Tank Radio	76
Tank Guns	77
Type 91 (1931) 6.5-mm Tank Machine Gun	77
Type 97 (1937) 7.7-mm Tank Machine Gun	78
Type 92 (1932) 13.2-mm Machine Gun	79
Type 94 (1934) 37-mm Tank Gun	80
Type 98 (1938) 37-mm Tank Gun	81
Type 1 (1941) 37-mm Tank Gun	82

CHAPTER I. JAPANESE ARMORED FIGHTING VEHICLES—Con.
Tank Guns—Continued.

	Page
Type 1 (1941) 47-mm Tank Gun	82
Type 90 (1930) 57-mm Tank Gun	83
Type 97 (1937) 57-mm Tank Gun	84
Type 94 (1934) 70-mm Tank Gun	85
Type 99 (1939) 75-mm Tank Gun (Experimental)	85

CHAPTER II. ARMORED TACTICS ... 86
  Introduction ... 86
    Organization of Armored Units ... 86
  Japanese Armored Tactical Principles ... 91
    Basic Doctrine ... 91
    Missions ... 91
    Formations ... 91
    Deployment in Two Lines ... 93
    Deployment in Two Echelons ... 94
  Tanks in Infantry Support ... 94
    Two Types of Cooperation ... 94
    Exploitation Operations ... 95
    Principles of Infantry-Tank Attacks ... 95
    Engineer Parties ... 96
    Orders for the Attack ... 96
    Use of Tanks Against Hostile Flanks ... 97
    Tank Regiment Tactics ... 97
    Tank Division Tactics ... 98
    Tanks in Close-Support Roles ... 99
    Example of Tank Division Tactics ... 99
  Infantry-Artillery-Tank Coordination ... 100
  Special Tank Operations ... 100
    Dawn Attacks ... 100
    Night Attacks ... 101
    Pursuit ... 101
    Tank-Versus-Tank Action ... 101
    Long-Range Raids ... 101
    Raids ... 102
  Tanks in Defense ... 102
  Summary ... 103

CHAPTER III. ANTITANK ARTILLERY ... 104
  General Estimate ... 104
  Infantry Weapons ... 106
    Critical Appraisal ... 106
    Type 94 (1934) 37-mm Gun ... 107
    Type 1 (1941) 47-mm Antitank Gun ... 109
  Field Artillery ... 116
    Adaptability of Field Artillery to Antitank Role ... 116
    Ammunition ... 116
    Type 90 (1930) 75-mm Field Gun ... 118

CHAPTER III. ANTITANK ARTILLERY—Continued.   Page
    Antiaircraft Artillery... 128
        Estimate in Antitank Role.. 128
        Use of Automatic Weapons in Antitank Role..................... 129
        Type 98 (1938) 20-mm Machine Cannon........................... 129
        Type 96 (1936) 25-mm Machine Cannon (Navy)................ 130
        Type 88 (1928) 75-mm Antiaircraft Gun............................ 135
        Type 10 (1921) 120-mm Dual-Purpose Gun (Navy)............ 137
    Coast Defense Artillery... 146

CHAPTER IV. ANTITANK MINES, RIFLE GRENADES, AND FLAME
    THROWERS.. 150
    Antitank Mines... 150
        Introduction.. 150
        Type 93 (1933) Mine... 151
        Type 93 (1933) Mine Fuze.. 152
        Yardstick Mine... 152
        Yardstick Mine Fuze... 153
        Type 98 (1938) Hemispherical Antiboat Mine.................. 154
        Plunger Contact Assembly.. 155
        Type 98 (1938) Antiboat Mine Fuze................................. 156
        Single-Horn Antiboat Mine (Tea-Kettle Mine).................. 156
        Plunger Contact Assembly.. 156
        Type 3 (1943), Model A, Land Mine (Pottery Mine)....... 157
        Type 3 (1943) Land Mine Fuze.. 158
        Type 3 (1943), Model B, Land Mine (Box Mine)............ 159
        Type 4 (1944) Land Mine... 160
        Shoulder-Pack Antitank Mine... 160
        Lunge Antitank Mine.. 160
        Concrete Mine... 162
        Sack-Type Mine... 162
        4-Kilogram Improvised Shaped-Charge Mine................... 163
        6-Kilogram Improvised Shaped-Charge Mine................... 163
        8-Kilogram Improvised Shaped-Charge Mine................... 163
        Type 3 (1943) Conical Hand-Thrown Mine..................... 164
        Coconut Land Mine... 166
        Experimental Hand-Thrown Mine.................................... 167
        Naval Depth-Charge Improvised Mine............................. 168
        Pole Charge... 169
        Type 99 (1939) Magnetic Demolition Charge................... 169
        Fuze... 170
        Suction-Cup Mine.. 171
        Tool-Box Mine... 172
        Mouse-Trap Mine.. 172

    Rifle Grenades... 172
        Type 2 (1942) 40-mm Hollow-Charge Rifle Grenade...... 172
        Type 2 (1942) 30-mm Hollow-Charge Rifle Grenade...... 173

    Flame Throwers.. 174
        Type 93 (1933) Flame Thrower.. 174
        Type 100 (1940) Flame Thrower...................................... 174

	Page
CHAPTER V. ANTITANK METHODS	175
General Doctrine	175
Employment of Antitank Guns	175
Selection of Positions	176
Large-Scale Antitank Defense	177
Tank Hunters	178
Methods of Attack	178
Combat Unit Teams	180
Tankborne Infantry	181
Engineer Assault Team	184
Assault Against Flame-Thrower Tanks	193
Individual Suicide Attacks	194
Antitank Obstacles	196
Ditches	198
Log Barricades	198
Posts	199
Abatis	199
Walls	199
Antitank Obstacles in Cities	200
Minefields	201
Common Minefield Sites	201
Mines in Manila	203
Methods of Laying Mines	206
Methods of Marking Minefields	210
Recent Antitank Methods	212
Antitank Methods in the Philippines	212
Antitank Methods on Okinawa	213

Chapter I. Japanese Armored Fighting Vehicles

Introduction

The Japanese produced their first modern light tank in 1935. This vehicle, the Type 95 (1935), subsequently was standardized and manufactured in large numbers. With its improved suspension and hull, and its turret-mounting of a Type 94 (1934) 37-mm high-velocity gun, it represented a considerable advance in Japanese design, which prior to 1935 was preoccupied with the production of imitations of 4- to 15-ton tanks purchased from other countries. Yet, in common with all early Japanese tanks, the protective armor of the Type 95 was made extremely light, with a maximum thickness of only 0.5 inch. From 1935 to 1942, in addition to the Type 95 light tank, the Type 97 (1937) medium tank, in both the original and improved versions, and the Type 2 (1942) amphibious tank were also developed and produced in considerable numbers.

The medium tank, known as the Type 97 (1937) and weighing approximately 15 tons, was produced in 1937. Its general design is satisfactory, but, as engagements with U. S. tanks have shown, its maximum armor thickness of only 1 inch is inadequate to withstand high-velocity projectiles. Furthermore, the turret-mounted 57-mm low-velocity gun, which is its primary armament, is unsuited for tank-versus-tank fighting.

Since the original Type 97 was produced, however, it has been modified by substitution of a high-velocity 47-mm gun in place of the 57-mm piece, and this new weapon should prove more satisfactory. Tanks of this new design have been encountered in Burma and in the Pacific theaters. Although the installation of the high-velocity gun necessitated the redesigning of the turret, the armor was not increased, nor was any other major improvement effected. Recent combat reports indicate, however, that the quality of the 47-mm AP projectile has been improved. Previously, tests showed that the metal was brittle and tended to break up.

Apart from the improved version of the Type 97 medium tank, the Type 2 (1942) amphibious tank, first encountered on Kwajalein, is the latest and only other known modern Japanese tank. While the method of flotation by means of detachable pontons is extremely interesting, the most significant trend in this type is the coaxial mounting of the Type 1 (1941) 37-mm gun and the Type 97 (1937) 7.7-mm machine gun in the turret. In no other vehicle have the

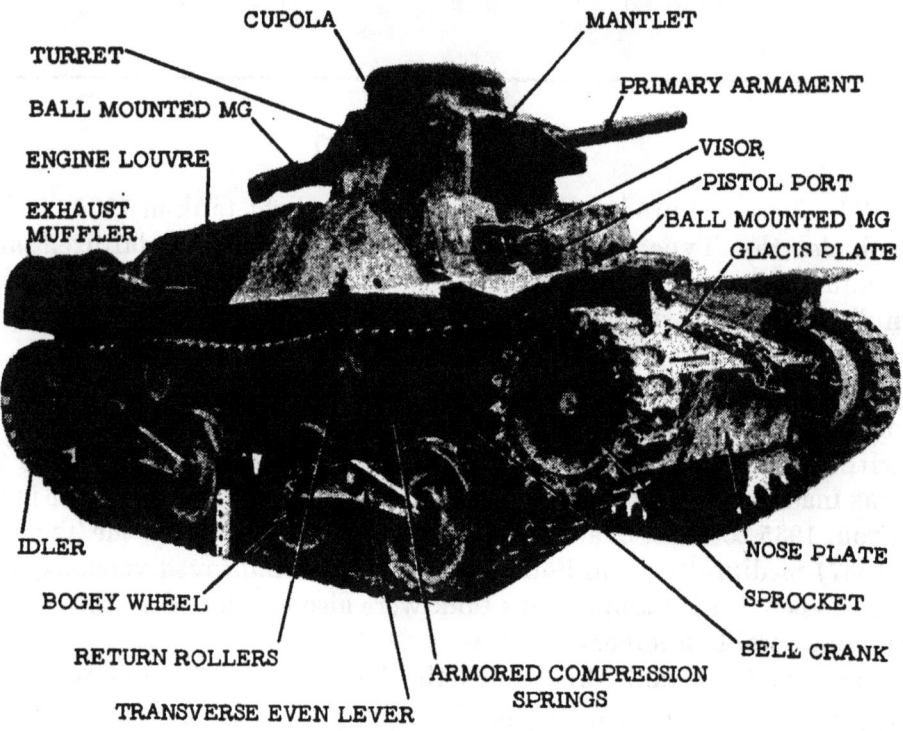

Figure 1.—Tank nomenclature.

Japanese been known to mount coaxially the primary and secondary armament. In addition, the chamber capacity of the 37-mm gun has been increased, indicating that it would have a somewhat higher muzzle velocity than previously encountered Japanese tank-mounted guns of this caliber. The hull design shows considerable improvement, particularly in the elimination of re-entrant angles. Yet the armor is consistently light, the maximum thickness varying from 0.47 to 0.52 inch on the sides of the turret.

Recent reports indicate that the Japanese may have developed a tank weighing approximately 30 tons with a long, high-velocity gun as its principal armament. Its maximum armor thickness is reported to be 2.92 inches, or 0.975 inch thicker than that of any armored vehicle encountered thus far. A maximum speed of 30 miles per hour is claimed.

There is also some evidence that the Japanese have developed two new light tanks. One is mounted on a Type 1 (1941) prime-mover chassis. It weighs about 20 tons, according to reports, and has a maximum road speed of approximately 20 miles per hour. The other tank, a 17-ton vehicle, is described as an improved Type 97 (1937) medium tank redesigned to carry the 75-mm gun. It is said to have a maximum armor thickness of 2.34 inches, with one plate 0.975 inch thick reinforced by another 1.365 inches thick.

Tankettes

Type 92 (1932) Tankette

The Type 92 tankette represents the earliest model still operational in the Japanese Army. This vehicle has the turret mounted to the rear of the chassis, giving it a boot-like appearance. Both welded and riveted construction are used throughout the hull. There is no protection against bullet splash at any of the vision slits and openings. Caliber .30 AP can penetrate the rear door at ranges up to 300 yards, while .50 caliber can penetrate front, sides, rear, and turret at ranges up to 600 yards. Suspension is four-point, with the use of bell cranks resisted by armored compression springs on each side. A front-

Figure 2.—Type 92 (1932) tankette, left side.

Figure 3.—Type 92 (1932) tankette, left front three-quarters, with tracked trailer.

Figure 4.—Type 92 (1932) tankette, front.

sprocket drive is used. There are four rubber-tired bogie wheels in pairs and two return rollers on each side. The tankette is very maneuverable, but sharp turns must be avoided as the outside guided track has a tendency to slip off during turns. Tracks are the outside center-guide type. The long, sloping glacis plate is a prominent identification feature. A light machine gun, ball-mounted in the turret, is the only armament.

Figure 5.—Type 92 (1932) tankette, left rear three-quarters.

APPROXIMATE SPECIFICATIONS:

Weight	3 tons.
Length	10 feet, 3 inches.
Width	5 feet, 3 inches.
Height	5 feet, 4 inches.
Clearance	13½ inches.
Crew	2 men.
Armor	6 to 14 mm (0.24 to 0.55 inch).
Armament	1 6.5-mm MG (ball-mounted).
Engine	4-cylinder, 32-horsepower.
Transmission	4 speeds forward, 1 reverse.
Ground contact	6 feet.
Width of track	5 inches.
Track pitch	3 inches.
Diameter of sprocket	21 inches.
Diameter of bogie wheel	15 inches.
Diameter of rear idler	15 inches.

Height to center of sprocket_____ 25 inches.
Performance:
    Speed_____ 25 miles per hour.
    Range of action_____ 100 miles.
    Gradient_____ 27°.
Obstacles:
    Trench_____ 4 feet, 6 inches wide.
    Step_____ 2 feet, 1 inch high.
    Ford_____ 2 feet deep.

Type 94 (1934) Tankette

The Type 94 tankette embodies the general design features of the Type 92, but the small rear idler on the latter has been replaced by a large trailing idler. The suspension is bell-crank resisted by armored compression springs. The engine is reported to be a Ford tractor motor of 32 horsepower. The vehicle is armed with one machine gun.

Figure 6.—Type 94 (1934) tankette.

The turret, constructed of rolled armor plate, is mounted on a ball race and forms a cover for the fighting compartment. It consists of a mantlet for the machine gun, a turret-traverse lock, an entrance hatch, two vision apertures, a gun-sighting aperture, and an aerial opening. The interior of the turret is lined with asbestos to afford protection from heat radiation. Since there is no provision for a traversing gear, traverse of the turret probably is accomplished by shoulder pressure against the machine gun, the ball mounting of which is constructed in two sections.

The hull is constructed of light armor plate. The inner surface of the plates surrounding the driving and fighting compartments is lined with asbestos which acts as a protective measure against heat radiation, both from the engine and the climate. On the inside of the front plate of the driving compartment, there are vision slits to the right and left; in front of the inner flap door there is another vision aperture fitted with bullet-proof glass. There is also a sighting and firing aperture for a small-arms weapon. In the front there is a square access plate which can be lifted for checking the transmission. During travel this is kept locked.

The engine and the gasoline tank are located in the fighting compartment. Thus the engine auxiliaries are readily accessible from the driver's seat. The engine itself appears to be decidely old fashioned in design; it has splash lubrication, for example. Design of the controlled differential steering is quite straightforward, but the differential housing is supported in plain bush bearings inside the sleeves of the control bevel wheels which, in turn, are carried in ball bearings in the walls of the brake housing. Separate taper roller thrust-bearings are provided. The steering brakes are of conventional toggle-operated two-shoe type. Since they are totally enclosed in a cast housing, it would be expected that trouble would arise from overheating.

The suspension of the tankette is a modification of the Carden-Lloyd type. It employs front-sprocket drive, a large trailing idler, and two return rollers. The four dual bogie wheels are resisted by armored compression springs. It would appear that the lateral rigidity of the bogie assembly would not be very great, and severe stresses might arise under adverse steering conditions.

The crew consists of two men: a driver and a machine gunner, who is also the tankette commander.

The tankette is armed with a ball-mounted Type 91, 6.5-mm machine gun and possibly one other light weapon.

APPROXIMATE SPECIFICATIONS:

Weight	3.4 tons
Length	11 feet.
Width	5 feet, 3 inches.
Height	5 feet, 4 inches.
Clearance	12 inches.
Crew	2 men.
Armor	4 to 12 mm (0.16 to 0.47 inch).
Armament	1 6.5-mm Type 91 tank MG.
Engine and power plant:	
Type	4-cylinder, air-cooled, in-line, gasoline.
Horsepower	32.
Normal engine speed	1,800 revolutions per minute.
Maximum engine speed	2,700 revolutions per minute.
Firing order	1—2—4—3.
Carburetor	"Tokiwa" Model NV. 41.

Engine and power plant—Continued.
- Fuel pump........................ "Autopulse" electric pump.
- Ignition.......................... Magneto and additional hand-operated impulse magneto (Model BH2).
- Generator........................ 12 volts, 75 watts.
- Starter........................... 12 volts, 1.4 horsepower.
- Battery.......................... Stowed on the right side behind the driver's seat; capacity 12 volts, 60 watt hours.
- Cooling.......................... Fan running at engine speed with cowl.
- Lubrication...................... Splash system, gear-type pump.
- Turret traverse.................. 360°.

Performance:
- Speed............................ 26 miles per hour.
- Range of action.................. 100 miles.

Obstacles:
- Trench........................... 4 feet, 6 inches wide.
- Step............................. No details.
- Ford............................. 2 feet deep.

Type 97 (1937) Tankette

The Type 97 (1937) tankette is a light mechanized reconnaissance vehicle powered by a 48-horsepower, 4-cylinder, air-cooled, valve-in-head Diesel engine. This tankette has a suspension practically the same as that of the Type 94 tankette. The hull and turret, however, have been completely redesigned. More room has been provided in the turret to accommodate a 37-mm tank gun. As an alternative,

Figure 7.—Type 97 (1937) tankette, left side.

a machine gun sometimes is mounted in place of the 37-mm weapon. This tankette shows a definite attempt on the part of the Japanese to design a simpler front plate and to improve the deflection angles of the armor. Its whole appearance evinces better design and cleaner features than its predecessors, the Types 92 and 94 tankettes.

The turret of the Type 97 is mounted on a ball race and is constructed of rolled armor plate. It has an all-around armor thickness of 0.39 inch. A Type 94 (1934) 37-mm tank gun or a Type 97 (1937) 7.7-mm tank machine gun is mounted in the turret which is lined with asbestos to protect the crew from heat radiation.

The hull is also made of armor plate, riveted and bolted together. The front plate has a thickness of 0.47 inch, and other armor thicknesses vary from 0.16 to 0.47 inch.

The engine, located in the fighting compartment, is a Diesel which reduces to some extent the fire risks involved in such location.

Suspension of the Type 97 tankette is a modified Carden-Lloyd. It employs front-sprocket drive, a large trailing idler, and two return rollers. The four dual bogie wheels are resisted by armored compression springs.

The crew consists of two men: a driver and a turret gunner, who is also the tankette commander.

DETAILED SPECIFICATIONS:

Weight	4.2 tons.
Length	12 feet.
Width	6 feet, 4 inches.
Height	5 feet, 11 inches.
Clearance	13½ inches.
Crew	2 men.

Armor:	mm	inch
Gun mantlet	--	----
Turret sides	10	0.39.
Turret top	8	0.31.
Hull front	12	0.47.
Hull glacis	4	0.16.
Hull nose	6	0.23.
Hull side	10	0.39.
Hull lower side	6	0.23.
Hull rear	10	0.39.
Hull top	8	0.31.

Armament	1 Type 94 (1934) 37-mm gun, or 1 Type 97 (1937) 7.7-mm tank MG.
Ammunition	54 rounds of 37-mm, or 1,200 rounds of 7.7-mm.

Engine and power plant:

Type	4-cylinder, air-cooled, valve-in-head, Diesel.
Horsepower	48.

Engine and power plant—Continued.
- Bore: 115 mm.
- Stroke: 150 mm.
- Compression ratio: 15.2.
- Standard revolutions per minute: 1,500.
- Maximum horsepower: 60 at 2,700 revolutions per minute.
- Valve clearance:
  - Intake valve: 0.20 mm (warm).
  - Exhaust valve: 0.25 mm (hot).
- Valve timing:
  - Inlet valve opens: At top dead center.
  - Inlet valve closes: 50° after bottom dead center.
  - Exhaust valve opens: 45° before bottom dead center.
  - Exhaust valve closes: 15° after top dead center.
- Fire order: 1—2—4—3.
- Ignition: Bosch model automatic.
- Generator: 24 volts, 300 watts.
- Storage battery: 12 volt, 120 ampere hours.
- Starter motor: 1 24-volt, 6-horsepower.
- Reduction gear: 3.05.

Steering: Clutch-brake.
Transmission: Conventional sliding gear type; 4 speeds forward, 1 reverse.
Brake system: Foot and hand-operated.
Fuel pump: "Ikegaki" type fuel-injection pump.
Fuel tank capacity: Main, 18.21 gallons; auxiliary, 8.45 gallons.
Cooling system: Air-cooled, 2 fans.
Clutch: Dry multiple-disc type.
Performance:
- Speed: 28 miles per hour.
- Range of action: 100 miles.

Obstacles:
- Ford: 32 inches deep.
- Trench: 5 feet, 8 inches wide.
- Step: No details.

Figure 8.—Type 97 (1937) tankette, left front three-quarters.

Figure 9.—Type 97 (1937) tankette, right side.

Figure 10.—Type 97 (1937) tankette, right front three-quarters.

Figure 11.—Type 97 (1937) tankette, front.

Figure 12.—Type 97 (1937) tankette, rear.

Figure 13.—Type 97 (1937) tankette, left rear three-quarters.

Figure 14.—Type 97 (1937) tankette, right rear three-quarters.

Figure 15.—Type 97 (1937) tankette, top.

Light Tanks

Type 93 (1933) Light Tank

This tank represents the early development of the light tank series. The box-type hull is divided into three compartments. The center compartment is the fighting compartment, the superstructure of which overhangs the tracks. The right-hand side of the front of this compartment is extended forward to form a sponson for the ball-mounted machine gun. In the forward compartment, the driver sits on the left, and the gunner on the right. Suspension is by six small rubber-tired bogie wheels mounted on three semi-elliptic springs on

Figure 16.—Type 93 (1933) light tank, left side.

Figure 17.—Type 93 (1933) light tank, left front three-quarters.

Figure 18.—Type 93 (1933) light tank, right front three-quarters (Photo is reversed).

each side. There are three return rollers on each side. This tank employs a front-sprocket drive, and has a center-guide track. The turret mounts one machine gun to the front, and some pictures show a similar weapon mounted to the rear of the turret. The turret is small, high, and rounded with tapered sides.

APPROXIMATE SPECIFICATIONS:

Weight	7.8 tons.
Length	14 feet, 8 inches.
Width	5 feet, 11 inches.
Height	6 feet.
Clearance	15 inches.
Crew	3 men.
Armor	Up to 22 mm (0.87 inch) (reported)
Armament	1 MG (hull); 1 MG (turret).
Steering	Clutch-brake.
Ground contact	10 feet.
Engine	6-cylinder, air-cooled, 85-horsepower, Mitsubishi, gasoline.
Cooling	Air.
Width of track	7½ inches.
Pitch of track	3½ inches.
Diameter of sprocket	1 foot, 6 inches.
Diameter of rear idler	1 foot, 3 inches.
Height of sprocket center	1 foot, 8 inches.
Performance:	
Speed	28 miles per hour.
Obstacles:	
Trench	5 feet, 8 inches wide.
Step	1 foot, 6 inches high.
Ford	2 feet, 8 inches deep.

Figure 19.—Type 93 (1933) light tank, front.

Type 93 (1933) Light Tank (Improved Version)

This tank is an improvement of the original Type 93. Although reported to be armed with a 37-mm gun, photographs show that the turret and hull have not been changed enough to accommodate such a weapon. The major change is in the suspension in which semi-elliptical springs have been replaced by the conventional Japanese light-tank suspension—bell-crank, resisted by armored compression springs. There are four bogies in pairs on each side and a large rear idler which acts as a bogie. Front-sprocket drive is employed.

Figure 20.—Type 93 (1933) light tank improved.

APPROXIMATE SPECIFICATIONS:

Weight	7.8 tons.
Length	14 feet, 8 inches.
Width	5 feet, 11 inches.
Height	6 feet.
Clearance	15 inches.
Crew	3 men.
Armor	Up to 22 mm (0.87 inch) (reported).
Armament	1 MG (hull), 1 MG (turret).
Engine	6-cylinder, 85 horsepower, air-cooled, Mitsubishi, gasoline.
Ground contact	9 feet, 6 inches.
Width of track	7½ inches.
Diameter of bogie wheel	15 inches.
Track pitch	3½ inches.
Steering	Clutch-brake.
Performance:	
Speed	25 miles per hour.
Range of action	120 miles.

Obstacles:
- Trench _____ 5 feet, 8 inches wide.
- Step _____ 1 foot, 6 inches high.
- Ford _____ 2 feet, 10 inches deep.

Type 95 (1935) Light Tank

The Type 95 (1935) light tank is a full-track combat vehicle. It is powered by a single six-cylinder Diesel engine of 90 to 110 horsepower. The armament consists of one Type 94 37-mm tank gun mounted in a steel turret and two Type 97 7.7-mm machine guns, one mounted in the turret, the other forward in the hull. The crew consists of three men: a driver, an engineer, and a turret gunner.

The turret is manually operated and may be traversed 360 degrees in either direction. It is riveted, bolted, and welded and has an all-around armor thickness of 0.47 inch. The top of the turret has two hatches which have an armor thickness of 0.35 inch.

The hull is riveted and bolted armor plate. On the front slope plate and on the engine-compartment covering, this plate is 0.25 inch thick; on all other parts of the hull it is 0.47 inch thick. There are two hatches on the front slope plate and a driver's hatch to the right of and below the turret. When the latter hatch is closed, the only vision devices provided for the driver and engineer are small vertical and horizontal slits.

The engine is located in the right rear of the tank, in a well-constructed compartment which is accessible from the driving compartment by a hatch that may be opened or closed from inside. This facility enables the engineer to work on the motor without getting out of the tank while under fire. The engine is air-cooled. Fuel and oil tanks are located at the rear of the engine compartment.

The engine is started by pulling the compression release lever on the right rear of the driver's seat and pressing the starter button on the dashboard. After the engine has started turning over, the compression release lever is pushed forward. Both hand and foot throttles are provided.

The all-steel tracks are driven by front-drive sprockets. There are two bogies, held together and resisted by a large armored compression spring, and four rubber-covered bogie wheels. The track is supported by two rubber-covered return rollers and a steel rear idler wheel. Tracks may be tightened by two ratchet wheels and lugs located on the right and left rear of the tank. The tracks are full-locking, enabling the tank to make turns in a radius of 8 feet.

Figure 21.—Rear of turret of Type 95 (1935) light tank. Note how turret overhangs superstructure making it easy to jam with brick or similar object.

Figure 22.—View of turret and superstructure of Type 95 (1935) light tank showing how a knife has been used to jam lower edge of turret against top of superstructure. Note pistol ports and vision slits marked with chalk.

Figure 23.—View of a knocked-out Type 95 (1935) light tank showing the two hatches in the glacis plate and the driver's hatch.

Figure 24.—View of right side of Type 95 (1935) light tank showing engine hatch open. Note also details of suspension.

Figure 25.—Type 95 (1935) light tank suspension in action.

Figure 26.—Track detail of Type 95 (1935) light tank showing track-adjusting nut and assembly.

Figure 27.—View through open glacis plate hatches of Type 95 (1935) light tank showing clutch-brake steering system. Note location of tank name plate.

Figure 28.—Interior of Type 95 (1935) light tank showing view through driver's hatch. Note ammunition stowage at right.

Figure 29.—Type 95 (1935) light tank with turret traversed to left showing interrelation of turret armament.

The driver's seat is on the right side of the tank, slightly forward of the center of the turret. The driver is concerned only with the driving of the tank under the instructions of the tank commander.

The engineer's position is to the left of the driver. In addition to his responsibility as engineer, he acts as bow gunner.

The turret gunner is tank commander. He carries on communications with other tanks by flags; the tank usually has no radio. He has a speaking tube through which he gives orders and relays instructions to the driver. He fires both the 37-mm gun and the turret machine gun, although the latter is not coaxially mounted.

The 37-mm gun is the principal armament. The gun may be elevated 24 degrees and depressed 20 degrees from the horizontal. It has a free traverse of 10 degrees right or left when the turret is stationary and is equipped with a telescopic sight (probably 8-power) graduated in 10-mil increments. The 37-mm gun fires HE and AP ammunition. Racks are provided inside the turret for the transportation of 119 rounds of ammunition. Cases for both types of projectiles are identical and are suitable for re-use.

The 7.7-mm machine guns are gas-operated, Bren-type guns, modified to be mounted in tanks. They are equipped with conventional open sights, and, in some cases, with telescopic sights. *These guns fire only rimless ammunition.*

The portion of the barrel forward of the mounting ring of the machine guns is enclosed in a hinged steel jacket to prevent injury to that part of the barrel which extends outside the tank. The shoulder piece is mounted on a pivot which allows it to be dropped out of the way when not in use. It is adjustable as to length and is held in one of four positions by a spring catch located on the under side of the stock.

Both guns can be elevated 25 degrees and depressed 10 degrees from the horizontal. The turret machine gun has a free traverse of 25 degrees in either direction; the hull gun has a free traverse of 35 degrees in either direction.

Besides the 37-mm gun and the two machine guns, tank personnel may be equipped with hand grenades. In a tank captured on Tarawa, the turret wall was fitted with cloth pockets which held eight grenades.

DETAILED SPECIFICATIONS:

Weight	Loaded, 16,800 pounds (approx. 85 percent stowed).
	Unloaded, 16,200 pounds (less ammunition).
Length	14 feet, 4.5 inches.
Width	6 feet, 9 inches.
Height	7 feet, 2 inches.
Clearance	1 foot, 3.5 inches.
Crew	3 men.

Armor:

	mm	inch	angle
Gun mantlet			
Turret front	12	0.47	
Turret sides	12	0.47	11°
Turret rear	12	0.47	7°
Turret top	9	0.35	90°
Hull front	12	0.47	90°
Hull glacis	9	0.35	72°
Hull nose	12	0.47	18°
Hull side	12	0.47	34°
Hull lower side	12	0.47	0°
Hull rear	12 to 6	0.47 to 0.23	26°
Hull top	9	0.35	90°
Hull floor	9	0.35	90°

Armament................ 1 37-mm Type 94 (1934) tank gun; 2 7.7-mm Type 97 (1937) MGs.

Ammunition.............. 119 rounds of 37-mm; 2,940 rounds of 7.7-mm.

Engine and power plant:
    Type.................. 6-cylinder, air-cooled, Diesel with overhead valves.
    Horsepower............ 110 at 1,400 revolutions per minute.
    Bore.................. 130 mm.
    Stroke................ 180 mm.
    Cooling............... Air, turbo-impeller type.
    Fuel pump............. Bosch-type.
    Generator............. 24-volt, Bosch-type with floating armature.
    Lubrication system.... Pressure from 3 oil pumps.
    Air cleaner........... Combination oil bath and filter.
    Fuel capacity......... 23 gallons, with 6 gallons reserve.
    Transmission.......... Straight, sliding gear, 4 speeds forward, 1 reverse.
    Final drive........... Double spur reduction.

Steering................ Clutch-brake.

Suspension.............. Modified Carden-Lloyd type, with one armored helical compression spring per side acting against bell cranks on each of two bogies.

    Height of track at sprocket. 2 feet, 7 inches.
    Center distance between sprocket and rear idler. 11 feet, 11½ inches.
    Diameter of sprocket (inside tooth diameter). 21½ inches.
    Diameter of bogie wheel.. 22½ inches.
    Diameter of rear idler... 21½ inches.
    Diameter of track support (or return) roller. 9¾ inches.
    Bogie tire size........ 570 mm by 70 mm.

Suspension—Continued.
- Track............................ Center-guide, steel blocks with dry pin. Tread (center to center) 5 feet, 11½ inches.
- Length of block...... 3¹³⁄₁₆ inches.
- Width of block....... 9¹⁵⁄₁₆ inches.
- Track contact with ground. 8 feet, 1½ inches.
- Ground pressure..... 8.7 pounds per square inch (approx.).
- Bridge class.......... 9.

Location of instruments and controls:
- Clutch pedal................ Operated by left foot.
- Accelerator................. Operated by right foot.
- Parking and stopping brake. Operated by right foot with hand lock.
- Steering levers............ Operated by right and left hands.
- Decompression lever..... Operated by right hand on hull.
- Tachometer................. On extreme left front dashboard, 0 to 2,400 revolutions per minute.
- Oil pressure gauge....... 0 to 7 kilograms per square cm.
- Headlight and generator switch. On panel to right of driver.
- Starter switch............. Push button on front panel.
- Speedometer.............. On front panel, 0 to 37.3 miles per hour.
- Ammeter................... On right panel, 0 to 30+.
- Temperature gauge...... In engine compartment, 0° to 120° centigrade.
- Oil pressure gauge....... In engine compartment, 0 to 7 kilograms per square cm.
- Oil temperature gauge.... In engine compartment, 0° to 120° centigrade.
- Gear shift lever.......... On transmission to left of driver.

Performance:
- Speed...................... 28 to 30 miles per hour.
- Range of action......... 90 to 110 miles.
- Gradient.................. 30° to 45°.

Obstacles:
- Trench.................... 6 feet wide.
- Step....................... 2 feet, 8 inches high.
- Ford....................... 3 feet, 3 inches deep.

The vulnerable points of this tank are: the underside of the sponson plate, the louvres on the right rear side of the engine compartment, and all vision slits throughout the vehicles.

The Type 95 tank is quite vulnerable to close-in attack with small weapons such as stick grenades and Molotov cocktails. It can be set afire; thus incendiary weapons are particularly valuable against this tank. *No weapon on the tank can be depressed lower than 20 degrees below the horizontal, thereby leaving a "dead space" extending 23 feet in all directions from the tank.* A man within this distance from the tank not only is in a favorable position to utilize his weapons, but is comparatively safe from fire by the tank itself.

Figure 30.—Type 95 (1935) light tank, left side.

Figure 31.—Type 95 (1935) light tank, left front three-quarters.

Figure 32.—Type 95 (1935) light tank, right side.

Figure 33.— Type 95 (1935) light tank, right front three-quarters.

Figure 34.—Type 95 (1935) light tank, front.

Figure 35.—Type 95 (1935) light tank, rear.

Figure 36.—Type 95 (1935) light tank, top.

Figure 37.—Type 95 (1935) light tank, left rear three-quarters showing stowage.

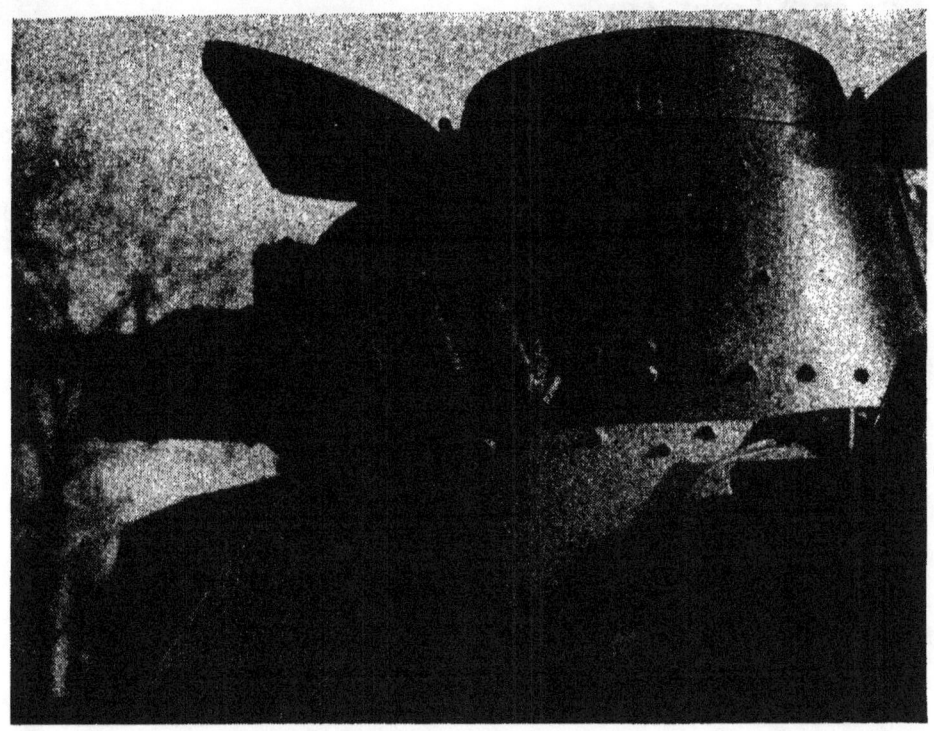

Figure 38.—Type 99 (1939) smoke dischargers mounted on left side of turret of Type 95 (1935) light tank.

Type 98 (1938) Light Tank

The Japanese have consistently referred to the Type 98 light tank in their documents. To date, no such vehicle has been captured. Documentary evidence, however, indicates that it is slightly similar to the standard Type 95 (1935) light tank.

DOCUMENTARY SPECIFICATIONS:

Weight	6.2 tons (metric).
Total length	13 feet, 6 inches.
Total width	7 feet.
Total height	5 feet, 11 inches.
Clearance	14 inches.
Crew	3 men.
Armor	6 to 12 mm.
Armament	1 37-mm tank gun; 2 7.7-mm tank MGs.
Ammunition	100 rounds 37-mm; 3,000 rounds 7.7-mm.
Type of engine	Air-cooled, 100-horsepower, 6-cylinder Diesel.
Fuel capacity	34.56 gallons.
Performance:	
Speed	31 miles per hour.
Gradient	Long 2/3.
Obstacles:	
Trench	6 feet, 7 inches wide.
Ford	31½ inches deep.

"Keni" Light Tank

It must be noted that the dimensions of this tank are very much like those of the Type 98 light tank, and it may be that this tank is a subsequent version of the Type 98. However, this tank is reported to be armed with a 47-mm tank gun and must be considered as a modern Japanese light tank. The armor is slightly heavier than that of the Type 98. The documentary evidence relating to the engine would indicate that this tank has a somewhat improved performance.

APPROXIMATE SPECIFICATIONS:

- Weight............ 7.6 tons.
- Length............ 13 feet, 6 inches.
- Width............. 7 feet.
- Height............ 5 feet, 11 inches.
- Belly clearance... 12 inches (also reported as 14 inches).
- Crew.............. 3 men.
- Armor............. 6 to 16 mm (0.23 to 0.62 inch).
- Armament.......... 1 47-mm tank gun; 1 7.7-mm MG.
- Engine............ 140 horsepower.
- Performance:
    - Speed......... 31 miles per hour.
    - Gradient...... 34°
- Obstacles:
    - Trench........ 6 feet, 7 inches wide.
    - Step.......... No details.
    - Ford.......... 2 feet, inches deep.

Medium Tanks

Type 89A (1929) Medium Tank

The oldest medium tank employed by the Japanese Army in the present war is the Type 89A (1929). This tank has a box-shaped hull which has a short front plate with a door on the right-hand side. Above this short front plate is a vertical front plate, with a machine gun protruding from the right side. There is a small hinged cupola on the top of the turret.

The suspension has nine small bogie wheels on each side with the leading ones independently mounted. There are five return rollers on each side mounted on a form of girder, and the vehicle is driven by the rear sprockets. The suspension is almost entirely covered by a protective skirting.

Power is furnished by a gasoline engine. A 57-mm low-velocity tank gun is the main armament, mounted in a turret capable of 360-degree traverse. In addition to the machine gun mounted in the front plate of the vehicle there is another mounted in the rear of the turret.

Figure 39.—Type 89A (1929) medium tank.

APPROXIMATE SPECIFICATIONS:

Weight	13 tons.
Length	19 feet, 3 inches.
Width	7 feet, 1 inch.
Height	8 feet, 6 inches.
Clearance	19 inches.
Armor	6 to 17 mm (0.24 to 0.67); also reported as 17 to 25 mm (0.67 to 0.98 inch).
Crew	4 men.
Armament	1 57-mm tank gun; 2 MGs.
Engine	136-horsepower, gasoline.
Ground contact	12 feet.
Width of track	12 inches.
Track pitch	6 inches.
Diameter rear sprocket	30 inches.
Diameter bogie wheel	9 inches.
Diameter front idler	36 inches.
Height to center of idler	33 inches.

Performance:
    Speed_____ 15 miles per hour.
    Range of action_____ 100 miles.
    Gradient_____ 34°.
Obstacles:
    Trench_____ 8 feet, 3 inches wide.
    Step_____ 2 feet, 9 inches high.
    Ford_____ 3 feet, 3 inches deep.

Figure 40.—Type 89A (1929) medium tank, with turret traversed so that machine gun is trained forward.

Figure 41.—Type 89A (1929) medium tank showing turret cupola. Note Navy insignia of anchor and chrysanthemum.

Type 89B (1929) Medium Tank

This tank is a modification of the original Type 89A (1929) medium tank. There are several important changes. The 89B has a longer front plate which is combined with the driver's front plate. The turret has been completely redesigned to accommodate a new type of cupola and to provide a more satisfactory aperture for the 57-mm tank gun. The gasoline engine has been replaced by a Diesel engine. Armor and armament, however, are the same as in the Type 89A.

APPROXIMATE SPECIFICATIONS:

Weight	13 tons.
Length	19 feet, 3 inches.
Width	7 feet, 1 inch.
Height	8 feet, 6 inches.
Clearance	19 inches.
Crew	4 men.
Armor	Same as Type 89A.
Armament	Same as Type 89A.
Engine	120-brake-horsepower Diesel.
Ground contact	12 feet.
Width track	12 inches.
Track pitch	6 inches.
Diameter of rear sprocket	30 inches.
Diameter of bogie wheel	9 inches.
Height to center of idler	33 inches.

Performance:
    Speed_____ 15 miles per hour.
    Range of action_____ 100 miles.
    Gradient_____ 34°.
Obstacles:
    Trench_____ 8 feet, 3 inches wide.
    Step_____ 2 feet, 9 inches high.
    Ford_____ 3 feet, 3 inches deep.

Figure 42.— Type 89B (1929) medium tank.

Type 94 (1934) Medium Tank

Although this tank is being reported as the Type 94 medium tank, there appears to be some doubt as to whether the type number is correct. The 57-mm gun has a free traverse of 20 degrees right and left and free elevation of −8 to +25 degrees.

Comparison with the Types 89A and 89B shows that the number of return rollers has been reduced to four, the girder has been removed, and the skirting redesigned. The long front plate has a door on the left, above which has been mounted a hull machine gun. The driver sits to the right. Power of the Diesel engine has been increased to 160 brake horsepower. With the above exceptions, the type 94 is practically identical with the Type 89B. This tank is often seen with a ditching tail.

APPROXIMATE SPECIFICATIONS:

Weight	15 tons.
Length (including ditching tail)	23 feet.
Width	7 feet, 1 inch.
Height	8 feet, 6 inches.
Clearance	19 inches.
Crew	4 men.
Armor	6 to 17 mm (0.24 to 0.67 inch).
Armament	1 57-mm tank gun; 1 hull MG and 1 rear turret MG.
Engine	160-brake-horsepower, air-cooled, Diesel.
Ground contact	12 feet.
Width of track	12 inches.
Track pitch	6 inches.
Diameter of rear sprocket	30 inches.
Diameter of front idler	36 inches.
Height to center of front idler	33 inches.
Diameter bogie wheel	9 inches.
Performance:	
Speed	18 to 20 miles per hour.
Range of action	100 miles.
Obstacles:	
Trench	9 feet wide.
Step	2 feet, 9 inches high.
Ford	3 feet, 3 inches deep.

Figure 43.—Type 94 (1934) medium tank, left side.

Figure 44.—Type 94 (1934) medium tank, left front three-quarters (Philippines).

Figure 45.—Type 94 (1934) medium tank, right side.

Figure 46.—Type 94 (1934) medium tank, right front three-quarters.

Figure 47.—Type 94 (1934) medium tank, left rear, showing ditching tail.

Figure 48.—Type 94 (1934) medium tank, right rear three-quarters (Philippines).

Figure 49.—Type 94 (1934) medium tank, top.

Type 97 (1937) Medium Tank

The Type 97 (1937) medium tank is a full-track armored vehicle, classed by the Japanese as a medium tank, although it fights at about the same weight as the U. S. light tank M5A1. It is powered by a V-12, air-cooled Diesel engine. The armament consists of one Type 97 (1937) 57-mm tank gun in the turret, one Type 97 (1937) 7.7-mm machine gun in the rear of the turret, and one Type 97 7.7 mm machine gun in the front superstructure. This 15-ton tank has a crew of four men: the tank commander, the turret gunner, the driver, and the hull machine gunner.

The manually-operated turret may be traversed 360 degrees right or left. It is constructed of bolted and riveted armor plate, 1.00 to 1.29 inches thick in front and 1.0 inch on the sides and rear. The top of the turret consists of a flat plate and a cupola with an armor thickness of 0.75 inch.

Figure 50.—Type 97 (1937) medium tank, left side.

The hull is also constructed of riveted and bolted armor plate, with a variation of thicknesses from 0.31 to 1.01 inches. The fighting compartment is lined with asbestos padding believed to be an insulation against heat. In most cases, two smoke generator-dischargers will be found on the glacis plate, one on the right and one on the left.

The engine is a V-12, air-cooled, valve-in-head Diesel with removable cylinder heads. There appear to be two different types of engines for this tank, one "A" which has been examined in captured tanks, the other "B" which is referred to in documents. (See detailed specifications.)

The suspension system consists of two bogies of two wheels each and an independently sprung bogie in the front and in the rear. These bogie wheels are rubber-tired, and are resisted by coil springs. There are three return rollers. Like other Japanese suspensions, this, too, is a modification of the Carden-Lloyd type.

The driver sits on the right side of the tank slightly forward of the turret, and drives the tank under the supervision of the tank commander.

The hull gunner sits to the left of the driver; in addition to being bow gunner, he acts as engineer.

The turret gunner and the tank commander ride in and fight from the turret. The tank commander controls the tank and carries on communication with other tanks by means of hand signals, flags, and in some cases radio.

The tank mounts a low-velocity Type 97 (1937) 57-mm tank gun in the turret, as well as one Type 97 (1937) 7.7-mm machine gun in a ball mounting to the rear of the turret. There is another Type 97 7.7-mm machine gun in the left front of the vehicle for the bow gunner.

In addition to the 57-mm tank gun and the two machine guns, recent Type 97 medium tanks have been found which mounted six smoke generator-dischargers, four on the right wall of the turret and

Figure 51.—Type 97 (1937) medium tank, right side.

one on each side of the front glacis plate. The smoke generators are of the carbon tetrachloride, base-emission type, and consist of a cardboard-covered metal canister. Burning time is estimated at about 2 minutes, and the distance of projection about 50 yards.

Figure 52.—Type 97 (1937) medium tank, right front three-quarters.

DETAILED SPECIFICATIONS:

Weight		29,685 pounds.	
Length		18 feet, 2 inches.	
Width		7 feet, 7 inches.	
Height		7 feet, 9 inches.	
Clearance		13½ inches.	
Crew		4 men.	
Armor:	mm	inches	angle
Gun mantlet			
Turret front	33	1.29	
Turret sides	26	1.0	11°.
Turret rear	26	1.0	11°.
Turret top	19	0.75	90°.
Hull front	25	0.98	11°.
Hull glacis	16	0.62	82° and 30°.
Hull nose	20	0.78	30° (thickness may vary 5 to 10 mm).
Hull side	26	1.0	25°.
Hull lower side	9	0.33	0°.
Hull rear	20	0.78	curved.
Hull top	13	0.51	90°.
Hull floor	8	0.31	90°.

Armament................ 1 57-mm Type 97 tank gun; 2 7.7-mm Type 97 MGs.
Ammunition.............. 121 rounds 57-mm; 3,825 rounds 7.7-mm.
Engine and power plant:
    Type.................... V-12, air-cooled, overhead-valve Diesel.
    Horsepower.............. 150 at 1,500 revolutions per minute.
Engine A (captured tank):
    Type.................... V-12, air-cooled, overhead-valve, Diesel. Removable cylinder heads. Cylinder heads, crank case, cooling fins, and clutch housing made of cast aluminum.
    Bore.................... 107 mm.
    Stroke.................. 166 mm.
    Piston displacement..... 17.9 liters (111.16 cubic inches).
    Maximum rated output... 150 brake horsepower (from a captured document).
    Injection and combustion chambers. Injector arranged directly over each piston; piston heads are recessed to form turbulence chambers.
    Cooling................. Centrifugal blowers.
Engine B (captured document):
    Type.................... V-12, air-cooled, overhead-valve, Diesel.
    Bore.................... 120 mm.
    Stroke.................. 160 mm.
    Swept volume (piston displacement). 21.7 liters (1,323.7 cubic inches).
    Compression ratio....... 17.8:1.
    Rated maximum power output. 170 brake horsepower.
    Normal power output.... 150 brake horsepower at 1,500 revolutions per minute.
    Firing order............ 1-12-5-8-3-10-6-7-2-11-4-9.
Valve clearances:
    Inlet valves............ 0.28 mm to 0.30 mm (cold).
    Exhaust valves.......... 0.30 mm (cold).
Valve timing:
    Inlet valve opens 20° before T. D. C.
    Inlet valve closes 40° after B. D. C.
    Exhaust valve opens 45° before B. D. C.
    Exhaust valve closes 15° after T. D. C.
Fuel system:
    Injector nozzles........ Closed overhead-type, automatic.
    Injection pressure...... 2,840 pounds per square inch.
    Injection pump......... Mitsubishi Type C.
    Fuel tank capacity:
        Main tank right 25.3 gallons.
        Main tank left. 26.4 gallons.
        Total.......... 51.7 gallons. Also 6 auxiliary tanks.
    Fuel consumption....... 3.7 gallons per hour at 9.3 miles per hour.
Lubrication system:
    Type.................... Force feed by gear pump.

Engine (B)—Continued.
    Lubrication system—Continued.

Normal pressure	3.56 to 56.9 pounds per square inch.
Instruments	Level, pressure, and temperature gauges.
Oil capacity	35 to 44 quarts (approx.).
Number of cooling fans.	4.

    Starting arrangements.... Electric starter motor and decompressing gear provided.

Electrical system:

Generator	24 volts, 500 watts.
Batteries	4 12-volt, 180 ampere hours.
Starter motor	24-volt, 6-horsepower.
Clutch	Dry, multiplate, similar to American tanks.
Reduction gear	A small, ribbed gear casing integral with the clutch housing contains 2 gears, giving a ratio of approximately 20:7 and also lowering transmission line by approximately 5 inches.

Transmission:

Type	Sliding pinion, with high-low transfer case.
Speeds	4 speeds forward, 1 reverse.

Steering:
    Reported to be a combination of epicyclic for normal steering and clutch-brake for skid turns. Control by steering levers.

Tracks:

Type	Single pin, open.
Width	12 inches.
Pitch	15 inches.
Number of links per tracks.	97.
Angle of approach	31°.
Angle of departure	24°.
Ground contact	12 feet, 2 inches.
Ground pressure	8.5 pounds per square inch.
Drive	Front-sprocket.

Driver's controls:
    Controls from right to left are: gear lever, transfer case lever, left steering lever, left skid-brake lever, clutch pedal, hand brake, foot brake, throttle, right skid brake lever, right steering lever. Also, left of the driver's seat: decompression lever; right of driver's seat: hand throttle.

Performance:

Speed	25 miles per hour.
Range of action	150 miles.
Gradient	30° to 45°.

Obstacles:

Trench	8 feet, 3 inches wide.
Ford	3 feet, 3 inches deep.

Figure 53.—Type 97 (1937) medium tank, front.

Figure 54.—Type 97 (1937) medium tank, rear.

Figure 55.—Type 97 (1937) medium tank, top.

Figure 56.—Type 97 (1937) medium tank, rear top view. Note differences from tank shown in top view (Figure 55).

Type 97 (1937) Medium Tank (Improved Version)

The improved version of the Type 97 medium tank is identical with the original Type 97 in many respects. As far as can be determined, the hulls of the original and the improved tanks are identical, and the modifications have been restricted to the turret. The width of the track on the improved version has been widened from 12 to 13 inches.

The turret has been changed from a generally circular type to a semirectangular overhanging type. This gives the turret a long, low appearance. The turret is 76 inches long and 56 inches wide at its widest point. There is no provision for a hand ring such as is provided on the original Type 97 medium tank. The mantlet is of the same general type as that used on the regular 97.

The change in the armament is another very important modification in this improved version of the Type 97. The low-velocity Type 97 57-mm tank gun has been replaced by the Type 1 (1941) 47-mm tank gun.

Figure 57.—Type 97 (1937) medium tank improved, left side.

As on the original Type 97, there are smoke candles mounted in racks on the side of the turret for use with the Type 94 self-projecting smoke candles. The racks are rigidly mounted on the turret in such a manner that a crew member can ingite the expelling charges in the bottom of the candle without exposing more than one hand and arm. The smoke candles must be manually ignited in the normal manner, as there is no provision for remote-control ignition. The candles are mounted at an angle of approximately 45 degrees, and tests have shown that these candles, as mounted on the launcher, have a range of approximately 300 yards.

Figure 58.—Type 97 (1937) medium tank improved, left front three-quarters.

Figure 59.—Type 97 (1937) medium tank improved, right side.

Figure 60.—Type 97 (1937) medium tank improved, right front three-quarters.

Figure 61.—Type 97 (1937) medium tank improved, front.

Figure 62.—Type 97 (1937) medium tank improved, rear.

Figure 63.—Type 97 (1937) medium tank improved, left rear three-quarters.

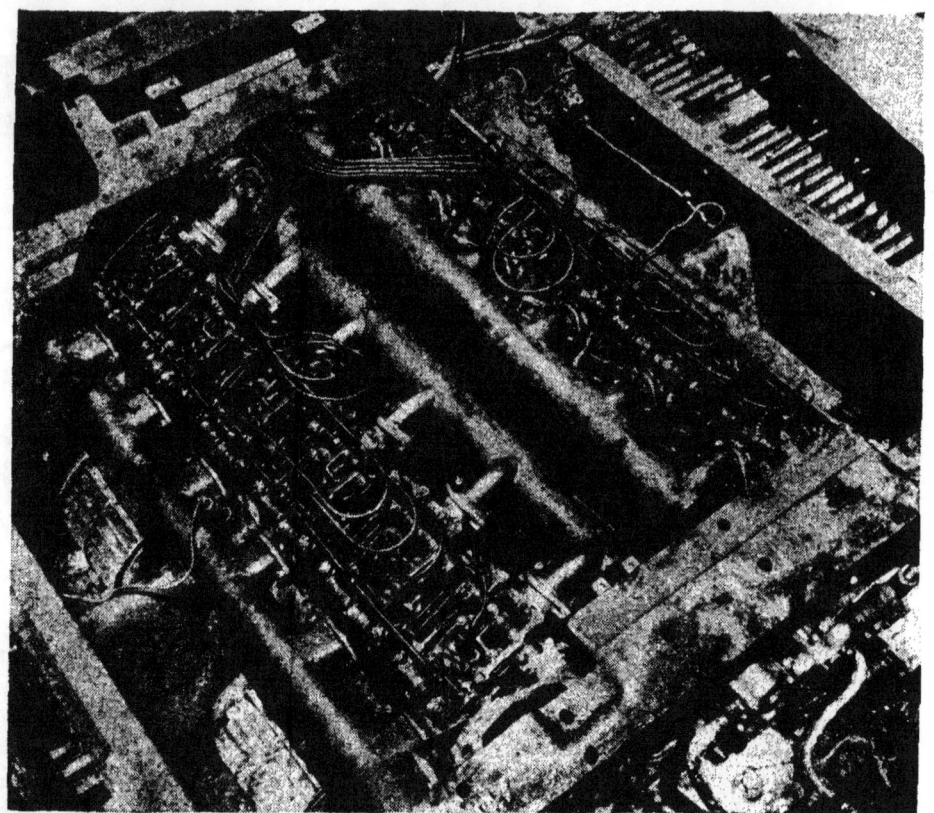

Figure 64.—Type 97 (1937) medium tank improved, view of engine.

Amphibious Tank

The Type 2 (1942) amphibious tank is a full-track amphibious vehicle for use in landing and in land operations. It is powered by a six-cylinder, air-cooled Diesel engine. It is armed with one 37-mm gun in the turret and two 7.7-mm machine guns, one of which is mounted forward in the hull and the other coaxially with the 37-mm piece. There is a crew of five men including a commander, a gunner, driver, hull machine gunner, and engineer.

The turret is constructed of rolled armor plate with an all-around thickness of 0.52 inch. The turret-hatch armor is 0.24 inch thick and is also constructed of rolled armor plate. There is one Type 1 (1941) or Type 94 (1934) 37-mm gun, and one Type 97 7.7-mm machine gun coaxially mounted in the turret.

The hull is constructed of rolled armor plate which is bolted and riveted together. The tank hull is not compartmented, and the engineer has working space completely around the engine except where the mounting is attached to the back of the hull. All openings up to

Figure 65.—Type 2 (1942) amphibious tank, left.

and including the turret ring are sealed with rubber. The armor of the hull is from 8 to 12 mm (0.32 to 0.47 inch) thick as shown in the detailed specifications.

The engine, located in the rear of the vehicle, is easily accessible because the hull is not compartmented. It is a six-cylinder, air-cooled Diesel. It drives the transmission through a transfer case arranged with two propelling shafts extending to the rear, one on each side of the engine. Engagement for water travel is made from a handle on the transfer case for each propeller. This transfer case also contains a built-in bilge pump for discharging hull leakage.

The suspension of this vehicle is a modification of the Carden-Lloyd type. It employs front-sprocket drive and two return rollers. The four dual bogie wheels and the trailing idler are resisted by armored compression springs located on the inside of the hull. The two track return rollers are mounted more forward than is usual in Japanese tanks.

The five-man crew, consisting of the tank commander, the gunner (turret), the driver, the hull machine gunner, and the engineer, all have designated positions. The tank commander is in complete charge of the vehicle and the crew. He rides in the turret with the turret gunner and gives instructions via a radio set which is installed in this vehicle in most cases. The engineer rides in the hull. The driver sits on the right front in the hull, and the bow, or hull, machine gunner sits to his left.

The 37-mm gun which is the primary armament of the vehicle may be elevated 5½ degrees and depressed 11½ degrees from the horizontal. It has a very limited, if any, free traverse when the turret is stationary. It is equipped with a telescopic sight. The weapon fires both HE and AP ammunition. There is ample storage space for machine-gun ammunition. Approximately 3,500 to 3,900 rounds may be expected to be the amount of 7.7-mm ammunition carried.

The machine guns are mounted in two ways. The hull machine gun is installed in a cast armor plate ball mount. The cast plate in this ball mount is one of the two places where rolled armor plate is not used; the other is the turret gun mantlet which is also cast. The second machine gun is mounted coaxially with the 37-mm gun—an innovation in Japanese tanks. The hull machine gun has a free traverse of 35 degrees in any direction. There is a provision for grenades to be carried in the vehicle.

There are two pontons constructed of ⅛-inch soft plate. The bow ponton weighs 2,300 pounds and is divided into six compartments with a total estimated volume of 220 cubic feet. The stern ponton weighs 1,515 pounds, with an estimated volume of 105 cubic feet. It incorporates twin rudders, 20 inches high, placed 16 inches forward of the rear ponton wall. The control is taken through a shaft into the hull by means of ⅜-inch cable. Steering in the water is accomplished by a horizontal handwheel at the tank commander's position in the turret. The pontons may be released from within the tank by the operation of handwheels controlling split-finger-type clamps.

Figure 66.—Type 2 (1942) amphibious tank, left front three-quarters, with pontons attached.

Figure 67.—Type 2 (1942) amphibious tank, rear with pontons attached.

Figure 68.—Type 2 (1942) amphibious tank, top view with pontons attached.

Figure 69.—Type 2 (1942) amphibious tank, waterborne.

Figure 70.—Removable spray-shield mounted on top of turret of Type 2 (1942) amphibious tank.

Figure 71.—Type 2 (1942) amphibious tank, releasing bow ponton.

Figure 72.—Type 2 (1942) amphibious tank, releasing stern ponton.

DETAILED SPECIFICATIONS:

Weight distribution:
    Weight with pontons _____ 24,915 pounds.
    Weight without pontons _____ 21,100 pounds.
    Weight front pontons _____ 2,300 pounds.
    Weight rear pontons _____ 1,515 pounds.
Length over-all _____ 24 feet, 4 inches.
Length without pontons _____ 15 feet, 10 inches.
Width _____ 9 feet, 2 inches.
Height _____ 7 feet, 8 inches.
Ground clearance _____ 14 inches.
Crew _____ 5 men.

Armor:	mm	inch	angle
Turret top	6	0.23	90°.
Turret rear	12	0.47	9°.
Turret sides	12	0.47	9°.
Turret front	12	0.47	9°.
Superstructure front	12	0.47	28°.
Hull nose	12	0.47	6° and 36°.
Hull glacis	6	0.23	83°.
Superstructure sides	10	0.39	0°.
Hull sides	10	0.39	0°.
Engine compartment sides	8	0.32	17° (approx.).
Rear deck	6	0.23	60°.
Belly plate	6	0.23	
Tail plate	10	0.39	10°.

Armament _____ 1 37-mm Type 1 tank gun; 2 7.7-mm Type 97 MGs.
Ammunition _____ 132 rounds of 37-mm.

Engine and power plant:
- Type — 6-cylinder, air-cooled Diesel with overhead valves.
- Horsepower — 120 at 1,400 revolutions per minute.
- Cooling — Centrifugal blowers.
- Fuel pump — Bosch-type.
- Generator — 24-volt, Bosch-type with floating armature.
- Fuel capacity — 53 gallons.

Transmission — Conventional sliding gear, 4 speeds forward, 1 reverse. High and low range transfer case.

Drive:
- On land — Front-sprocket.
- In water — Twin propellers behind lower tail plate which may be disengaged separately to assist steering.

Steering:
- On land — Clutch-brake.
- In water — Rudder and propeller.

Suspension — 2 bogies and trailing idler are mounted to compression springs located within the hull.
- Distance between track centers. — 8 feet, ¼ inch.
- Distance between sprocket and rear idler. — 12 feet, 8 inches.
- Diameter of rear idler — 26 inches.
- Diameter of bogie wheel — 22 inches.
- Diameter of front sprocket. — 19½ inches.
- Diameter of return roller — 12 inches.
- Height of sprocket to ground. — 2 feet, 5 inches.
- Track — Steel, link and pin engaging with 4 and 3 points.
  - Length over-all — 32 feet +.
  - Ground contract — 10 feet, 10 inches.
  - Length of link — 3.7 inches.
  - Width — 12 inches.
  - Angle of approach — 56.25°.
  - Angle of departure — Arcuate, on circumference of rear bogie idler.
- Bridge class — 18.

Driver's controls:
From left to right; gear shift lever, high and low range lever, left propeller shaft engaging lever, reverse propeller shaft lever, right propeller shaft engaging lever, left steering clutch, hand brake, foot brake, foot throttle, right steering lever, hand throttle, and decompression lever.

Escape hatches:
    Turret_____ 1 each side, size 22 by 18 inches.
    Hull_____ 2 in belly in rear of driver and hull gunner, size 15 by 10.5 inches.

Pistol ports:
    Turret_____ 3 in each side and 1 in rear.
    Hull_____ 1 in each corner.

Vision:
    Driver_____ Slit, size 4 inches by 1 inch.
    Hull gunner_____ Slit, size 4 inches by 0.125 inch.
    Commander and turret gunner. 2 slits, size 4 inches by 0.125 inch; 2 vision ports, 3.75 inches in diameter to right and left of 37-mm gun.

    The slits each have a bracket for clamping splinter-proof glass behind them or for sealing the tank against entry of water. The vision ports in the turret front have provision for at least 3 inches of safety-glass windows.

Water seals_____ Rubber seals around all openings up to and including the turret ring.

Pontons:
    Bow ponton:
        Weight_____ 2,300 pounds.
        Method of attachment. Attached to the hull by 3 clamps: 1 top center between driver and hull machine gunner; 2 on nose plate approximately 2.5 feet in toward center from each side.
        Appearance_____ Bow of a flat-topped barge with many odd angles at points of contact.
        Construction_____ Welded 0.125-inch plate (not armor). Nose section reinforced slightly by additional thickness of plate.
        Compartments_____ 6.
        Maximum height_____ 47 inches.
        Maximum length_____ 127 inches.
        Maximum width_____ 110 inches.
        Cubic volume_____ Estimated at 220 cubic feet.
    Stern ponton:
        Weight_____ 1,515 pounds.
        Method of attachment. Attached to the hull by 4 clamps in the sloping rear walls of the panniers.
        Compartments_____ 5.
        Maximum height_____ 44 inches.
        Maximum length_____ 85 inches.
        Maximum width_____ 110 inches.
        Cubic volume_____ Estimated at 105 cubic feet.

Provision for use on water:
    An airduct in the form of a square section chimney may be fitted over the air inlet grille in the center of the rear deck and a circular spray guard is fitted to the top of the turret over the hatch opening in some cases.

Performance:
     Maximum speed on land__ 23 miles per hour.
     Maximum speed afloat_____ 6 miles per hour.
Obstacles:
     Trench_____ 6 feet, 7 inches wide.
     Step._____ 2 feet, 5 inches high.
Radius of action:
     Land_____ 124 miles.
     Afloat_____ 93 miles.

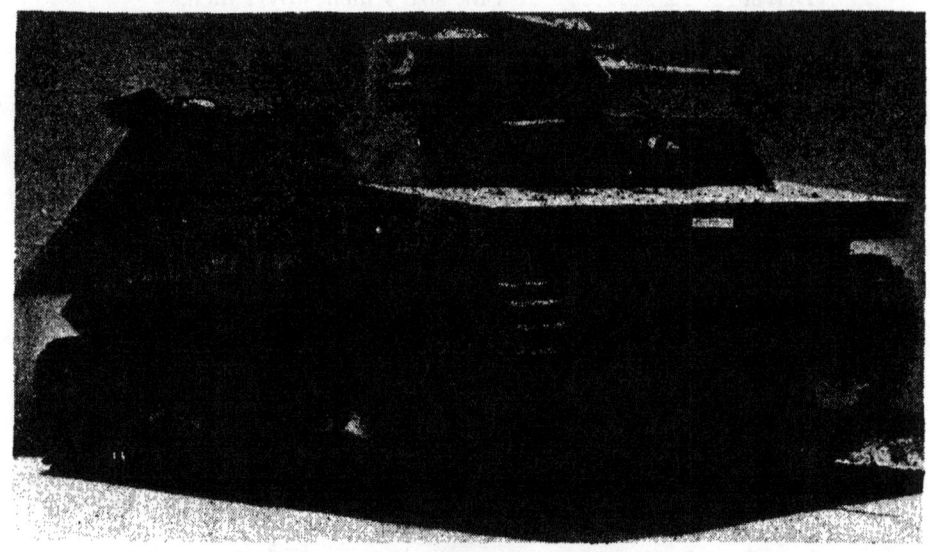

Figure 73.—Type 2 (1942) amphibious tank, right front three-quarters without pontons.

Figure 74.—Type 2 (1942) amphibious tank, right rear three-quarters without pontons.

Flame-Throwing Tanks

Flame-Throwing Tanks on Luzon

Eight Japanese flame-throwing tanks have been captured on Luzon. All were the same basic vehicle, but two versions were distinguished. In one version the 9 fuel tanks were externally mounted, while in the other the fuel tanks were mounted inside the vehicle. Armament of the versions also differed. The vehicle with exterior fuel tanks had one Type 97 (1937) 7.7-mm machine gun in the front-center position, and another similar weapon in the left front corner. It had one flame thrower in the right front corner and one in the right rear. (A variant was noted wherein the left front machine gun was replaced by another flame thrower.) The tank with interior fuel tanks had one machine gun in the front-center position and one flame thrower in the right front corner. Two flame throwers were also mounted on each side of the vehicle.

Both versions have 1-inch frontal armor, with ½ inch on the sides and ¼ inch on top. The vehicles are full-tracked and have very low silhouettes. Suspension differs from any previously encountered Japanese design. There are eight 10-inch bogie wheels on each side, bell-cranked, mounted in pairs and resisted by four 13-leaf springs on each side. Both versions are rear-sprocket driven and have front idler wheels. The version with exterior fuel tanks has three return rollers on each side; the one with interior tanks has but two on each side. Both versions are powered by 6-cylinder, air-cooled Diesel engines.

Tops of both versions are flat, with the exception of a so-called "conning tower" in front. This tower, about 36 inches in diameter, is 5 inches high and is covered by a swinging two-piece hatch. There is also an escape hatch, about 24 by 15 inches, in the top at the right rear corner.

It is noteworthy that the vehicles are equipped with a power winch in the rear, possibly used for removal of obstacles, or to move equipment. The large forks (see photograph) apparently are used for digging up mines in the path of the vehicles, but they also may be used for the destruction of barbed-wire entanglements. An electrical intercommunication system, with fixed microphone, is installed in each vehicle, and provision is made for external charging of the battery.

Either long or short flame throwers are used. Both types are ball-mounted, allowing for 20 degrees total traverse and an elevation of from minus 5 to plus 10 degrees. Ignition of both long and short types is accomplished by carbon arcs.

Machine guns of all vehicles examined were the Type 97 (1937) 7.7-mm light machine gun, ball-mounted, with total traverse of 20 degrees and elevation of from minus 5 to plus 10 degrees.

TENTATIVE SPECIFICATIONS (BOTH VERSIONS):

Over-all length	17 feet, 6 inches.
Height (excluding tower)	5 feet, 4 inches.
Over-all width	7 feet.
Width of track	11 feet, 6 inches.
Ground contact of track	15 feet, 6 inches.
Steering	Clutch-brake and epicyclic.
Maximum road speed	25 miles per hour.

Figure 75.—Flame-throwing tank with interior fuel tanks, and obstacle or mine removing fork raised.

Figure 76.—Flame-throwing tank with interior fuel tanks, right side, with obstacle or mine removing forks raised.

Figure 77.—Flame-throwing tank with exterior fuel tanks, front view, showing flame thrower on right of superstructure, with machine-gun mount in center, driver's hatch on left, and flame thrower on left side behind driver.

Figure 78.—Flame-throwing tank with exterior fuel tanks, left side, showing rear cylindrical tank and flame thrower in left front corner of superstructure behind driver.

Figure 79.—Flame-throwing tank with exterior fuel tanks, right side.

Self-Propelled Guns

Self-Propelled 15-cm Howitzer

The Type 38 (1905) 15-cm howitzer mounted on a medium tank chassis has been identified. It is not known definitely whether the tank chassis is the Type 97 (1937) medium tank or the Type 97 (1937) medium tank improved. The width of the track, however, would indicate that it is the latter.

The armor is assembled by riveting in the characteristic Japanese fashion. The armor on the chassis is the same as for the tank, with a maximum armor thickness of approximately 1 inch. The gun shield has 1-inch frontal armor and ½-inch side armor. There is also an armored shield on top of the side gun shields, but this does not appear to extend far enough to the rear to provide protection for personnel operating the howitzer. The vehicle has the standard V-12, air-cooled, Diesel tank engine, and the Type 97 medium tank suspension.

CHARACTERISTICS:

Length	18 feet, 2 inches.
Width	7 feet, 6 inches.
Chassis height	47 inches.
Height of shield	61 inches.
Over-all height	93 inches.
Diameter drive sprocket	28 inches.
Width of track	13 inches.
Ground contact	160 inches (approx.).
Diameter rear idler	28 inches.
Diameter bogie wheels	23 inches.

Figure 80.—*Type 38 (1905) 15-cm howitzer mounted on Type 97 (1937) medium tank chassis, left side.*

Figure 81.—Type 38 (1905) 15-cm howitzer mounted on Type 97 (1937) medium tank chassis, right front three-quarters.

Figure 82.—Type 38 (1905) 15-cm howitzer mounted on Type 97 (1937) medium tank chassis, rear view.

Figure 83.—Type 38 (1905) 15-cm howitzer mounted on Type 97 (1937) medium tank chassis, right rear three-quarters showing ammunition stowage box located above engine.

Figure 84.—Type 38 (1905) 15-cm howitzer mounted on Type 97 (1937) medium tank chassis, showing breech of piece and stowage of projectiles under floor of fighting compartment.

Type 2 (1942) 75-mm Self-Propelled Gun

This weapon is believed to be the Type 90 (1930) 75-mm field gun mounted on the Type 97 (1937) improved medium tank chassis. The weapon has been subject to considerable modification, however, in that the muzzle brake, common to the field piece, has been removed and replaced by a muzzle reinforcing ring. The horizontal sliding breechlock is somewhat smaller than that of the field gun. The

Figure 85.—Type 2 (1942) 75-mm self-propelled gun.

Figure 86.—Type 2 (1942) 75-mm self-propelled gun, as captured on Luzon.

Figure 87.—Type 2 (1942) 75-mm self-propelled gun showing hillside emplacement on Luzon.

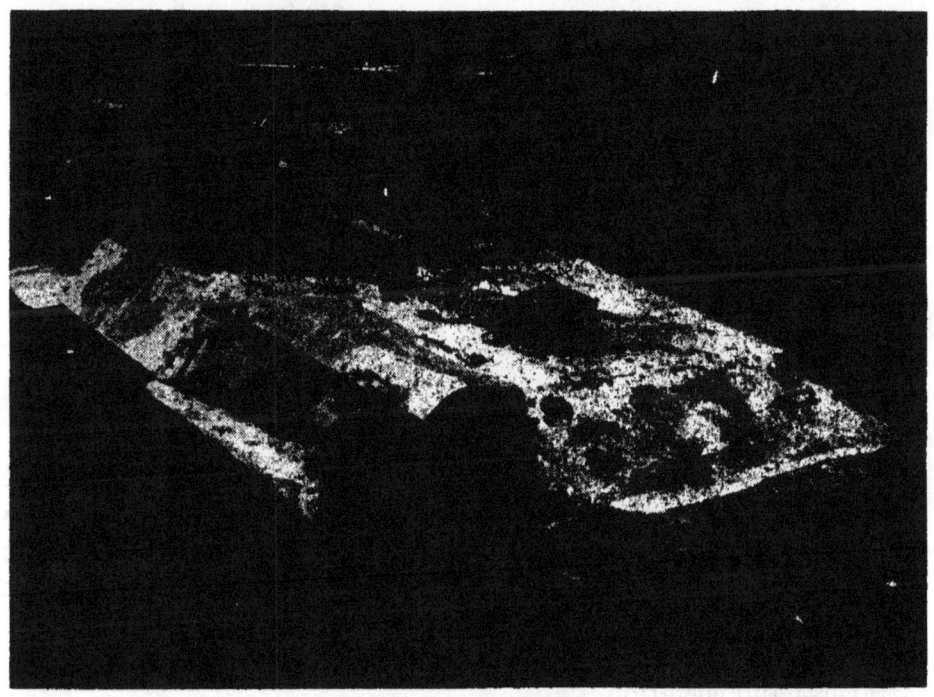

Figure 88.—Type 2 (1942) 75-mm self-propelled gun, showing interior of fighting compartment. Note mount for panoramic telescope, and modification of cradle compared to the Type 90 75-mm gun.

weapon apparently is designed for use as a tank destroyer, a light assault gun, and as self-propelled artillery. It uses the same ammunition as the field gun. The mounting of the gun on the Type 97 medium tank chassis provides excellent mobility, as this vehicle is capable of speeds up to 25 miles per hour. Since the vehicle has only about half the ground pressure of the U. S. M4A3 medium tank, it is capable of maneuver over unfavorable terrain.

In contrast to the Type 38 15-cm self-propelled howitzer, the self-propelled gun appears to be provided with an interior mantlet. It is also provided with an armored recoil mechanism and can probably be operated safely under frontal small-arms fire. The fighting compartment of the vehicle shows a decided trend on the part of the Japanese towards heavier armor. Whereas the frontal armor on the Type 97 improved medium tank, the most heavily armored vehicle encountered to date, is 25 mm (0.98 inch) the front of the fighting compartment of the self-propelled gun has 2 inches of armor. This is achieved by bolting additional plates of 1-inch armor to the front of the fighting compartment, the basic frontal armor of which is 1 inch thick.

SPECIFICATIONS:

Caliber	75 mm (2.95 inches).
Total traverse	10° (estimated).
Maximum elevation	25° (estimated).
Depression	5° to 7° (estimated).
Length of tube and breech ring	9 feet, 4 inches.
Length of tube	8 feet, 9 inches.
Length of rifling	88 inches.
Length of chamber	17.0 inches.
Width of breechblock	8.25 inches.
Thickness of breechblock	5.0 inches.
Length of sleigh	88.25 inches.
Length of recoil cylinders	54.5 inches.
Maximum recoil (from recoil scale)	75 cm (29.5 inches).
Number of lands	28.

105-mm Self-Propelled Weapons

It may be expected that several of the field pieces of this caliber will be modified for use in self-propelled roles. The current trend will find the Type 97 (1937) improved medium tank chassis used as the gun carriage for the weapons. If 105-mm self-propelled weapons are constructed in the manner in which the others have been made, the effectiveness of the weapon may be cut down by the limitations of traverse and elevation.

Armored Cars

Type 92 (1932) Navy Armored Car

This vehicle is easily distinguished as a naval-type armored car by the flag painted on the outside. All vehicles used by naval and marine forces are usually marked in this manner. There are six disc wheels with pneumatic tires. The vehicle has semi-elliptic springs. There are auxiliary wheels to prevent bellying when the vehicle is crossing rough terrain.

APPROXIMATE SPECIFICATIONS:

Weight	7 tons.
Length	15 feet, 9 inches.
Width	5 feet, 11 inches.
Height	7 feet, 6 inches.
Ground clearance	16 inches.
Crew	4 men.
Armament	4 to 5 LMGs.
Armor	8 to 11 mm (0.32 to 0.43 inch).
Engine	6-cylinder, 85-horsepower, water-cooled, gasoline.
Speed	50 miles per hour.

Figure 89.—Type 92 (1932) Navy armored car.

Type 93 (1933) "Sumida" Armored Car

This vehicle may be used as an armored railway car or on roads. It is equipped with flanged tires for use on railroad tracks and rubber-tired wheels for ordinary highway use. To change it from a rail to a road vehicle there are four built-in jacks, two in front and two in the rear of the vehicle. When traveling, the set of tires not in use is attached to the side of the vehicle. The engine is in the front, and there is a round cupola on the van-shaped hull. The road speed is estimated at about 25 miles per hour, but when on rails it is believed that the vehicle can attain speeds approximating 40 to 45 miles per hour.

APPROXIMATE SPECIFICATIONS:

Weight	7.5 tons.
Length	21 feet, 6 inches.
Width	6 feet, 3 inches.
Height	9 feet, 8 inches.
Ground clearance	16 inches.
Crew	6 men.
Armament	1 MG mounted in turret. Slits for rifles or LMGs.

Figure 90.—Type 93 (1933) "Sumida" armored car for road travel.

Figure 91.—Type 93 (1933) "Sumida" armored car for rail travel.

Figure 92.—Type 92 (1932) Army "Osaka" armored car reported as having been encountered in Burma.

Figure 93.—Vickers-Crossley Model 1925 armored car. This obsolete type may still exist.

Tank Radio

An examination of approximately 50 medium tanks, 12 light tanks, and miscellaneous other vehicles yielded the following information:

1. All medium tanks (Type 97 and Type 97 improved) were equipped with radio.
2. At least some of the light tanks were radio equipped.
3. The majority of the Type 97 and Type 97 improved medium tanks were equipped with Type 96 Mark 4E radio sets. Some of the Type 97 medium tanks were equipped with Type 147 radio sets.
4. Some of the light tanks were equipped with the Type 96 Mark 4E radio set, others with Type 306 radio sets.
5. One Type 147 radio set was found in a civilian passenger car.

6. One Type 97 medium tank which had been equipped with a Type 306 radio set had a makeshift antenna installed on the turret. This antenna would indicate operation of moderately high frequency (e. g. in the vicinity of 30 megacycles which would be consistent with the frequency range of the Type 306 radio set (20 to 30 megacycles), as determined from the calibration chart taken from the tank.

Examination of 12 other Type 97 improved medium tanks and one light tank disclosed the following information:

1. Five different types of radio sets were found in these tanks. The types were: Type 142, Type 147, Type 96 Mark 4E, Type 305, and Type 306 radio sets.

2. The Type 142, Type 147, and Type 96 Mark 4E are medium-frequency sets, e. g. below 10 megacycles, whereas the Type 305 and Type 306 are in the frequency range of 20 to 30 megacycles. The two latter types may be frequency modulated, but this could not be definitely ascertained in the field since none of the sets was in operating condition.

Tank Guns

Type 91 (1931) 6.5-mm Tank Machine Gun

This gas-operated, air-cooled, hopper-fed weapon is the old Type 11 (1922) 6.5-mm machine gun modified to be tank-mounted by the removal of the bipod. It is equipped with a blade front sight and a V-notched rear leaf sight sliding on a ramp. There is no windage or drift adjustment. The safety lever is turned down to a vertical position to make the weapon safe.

CHARACTERISTICS:

Caliber	6.5 mm (0.256 inch).
Weight	23.1 pounds.
Length over-all	43.5 inches.
Length of barrel	19.15 inches.
Maximum (cyclic) rate of fire	500 to 600 rounds per minute.
Cooling	Air.
Sights	Open V rear sight graduated from 300 to 1,500 mils. Blade front sight.
Feed	Clip-fed hopper on left holding 6 clips of 5 rounds each.
Provision for single-shot fire	None.
System of operation	Gas.
Ammunition	6.5-mm semirimmed S. A. A.
Muzzle velocity	2,440 feet per second.

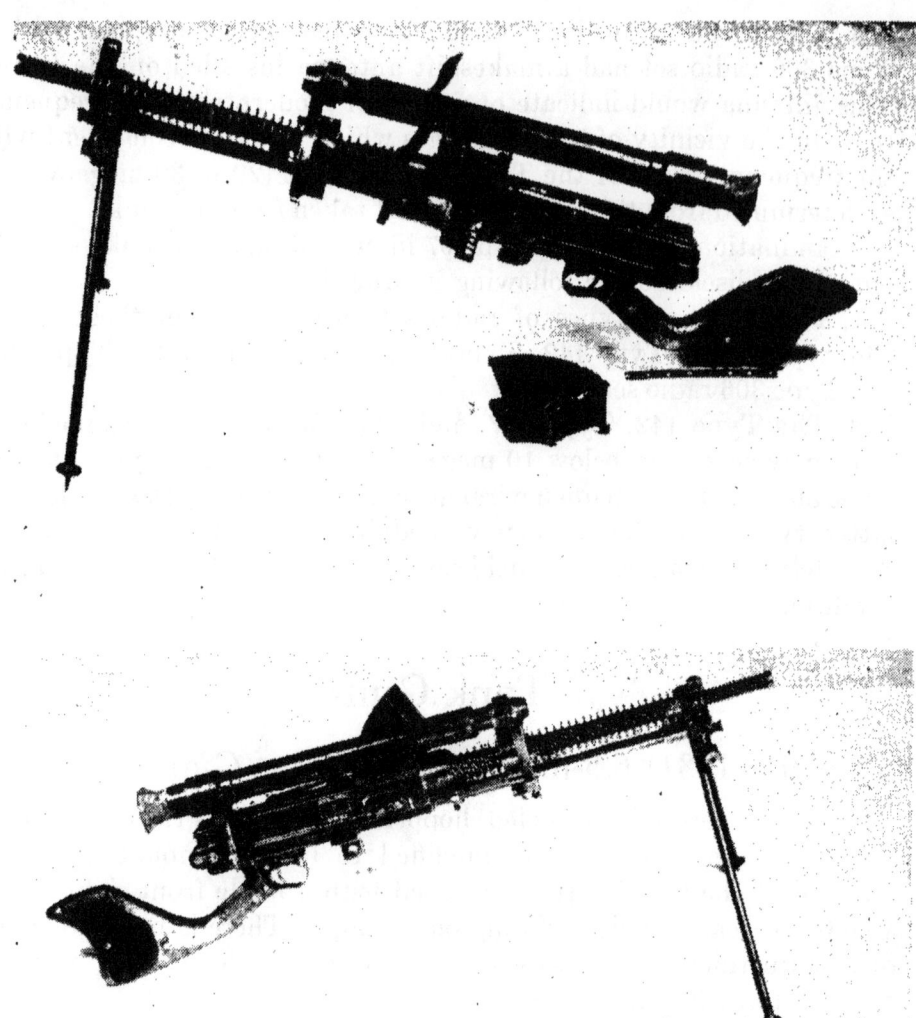

Figure 94.—*Type 91 (1931) 6.5-mm tank machine gun fitted with bipod for ground use.*

Type 97 (1937) 7.7-mm Tank Machine Gun

The Type 97 (1937) 7.7-mm tank machine gun is the standard machine gun in all recent Japanese tanks. A shoulder-controlled weapon, it is fitted with a pistol grip and adjustable stock. It is gas-operated and air-cooled. No provision is made for semiautomatic fire. In addition to the iron sights, a telescopic sight of 1.5-power and 30-degree field of view is usually fitted. To prevent injury to the gunner, a heavy rubber eye pad is attached to the rear of the telescopic sight. By the addition of a bipod, this weapon may be converted to ground purposes.

CHARACTERISTICS:

Caliber	7.7-mm (0.303 inch).
Weight	25.2 pounds without accessories.
Length with stock fully extended	47 inches.
Barrel length	28 inches.
Feed	30-round, vertical, box magazine.
Sights	Blade front sight and aperture back sight.
Muzzle velocity	2,375 feet per second.
Cyclic rate of fire	500 rounds per minute.
Ammunition	Rimless: Ball, AP, Tracer [same as is fired by the Type 99 (1939) 7.7-mm rifle and LMG].

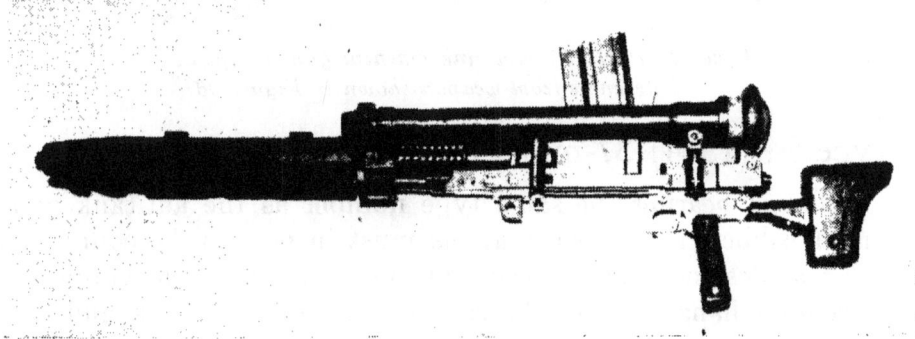

Figure 95.—Type 97 (1937) 7.7-mm tank machine gun with jacket guard, telescope, and magazine in place.

Figure 96.—Type 97 (1937) 7.7-mm tank machine gun showing appearance of fore end without guard.

Type 92 (1932) 13.2-mm Machine Gun

The Japanese refer to this gas-operated, air-cooled, magazine-fed weapon as the "13.2-mm vehicular machine gun." Documents state that it is designed for use as the primary armament of armored cars. Although no reliable information is available concerning this weapon, it is believed to be of Hotchkiss design and, therefore, probably closely resembles the Type 93 (1933) 13.2-mm machine gun in both performance and general characteristics.

Figure 97.—Type 97 (1937) 7.7-mm tank machine gun in typical ball mount. Note differences from weapon shown in Figure 96.

Type 94 (1934) 37-mm Tank Gun

Although bearing the same type number as the antitank gun of similar caliber, these two weapons must in no way be confused, as each was designed for a specific purpose. In addition, ammunition is *not* interchangeable, as the cartridge case of the tank gun is but 5.27 inches long. This gun is the primary armament of some Japanese light tanks, particularly the Type 95 (1935). There is some evidence that it may also be mounted in a tankette.

The gun is mounted in the tank turret at approximately its center of gravity. A form of gimbal mounting is used having vertical trunnions, which provide for a limited degree of independent free traverse, in addition to the usual horizontal trunnions for elevation and depression. The main traverse, of course, is obtained by rotating the turret. Traverse and elevation are both controlled by means of an adjustable shoulder rest attached to the left side of the cradle. The pistol grip, the trigger, and a telescopic sight are arranged on the left of the gun.

CHARACTERISTICS:

Caliber	37-mm (1.46 inches).
Weight of gun and cradle	305 pounds.
Over-all length of gun and mount	62.5 inches.
Over-all length of gun	53.9 inches.
Length of tube	49.5 inches.
Breechblock	Semiautomatic vertical sliding.
Recoil system	Hydrospring.
Ammunition	AP and HE.
Muzzle velocity	1,900 feet per second.
Armor penetration	1.4 inches at 300 yards normal impact.

Figure 98.—Type 94 (1934) 37-mm tank gun.

Figure 99.—Type 94 (1934) 37-mm tank gun in turret mount on Type 95 (1935) light tank.

Type 98 (1938) 37-mm Tank Gun

This weapon has recently been recovered, but a complete report has not yet been made. The gun was first found mounted in a "Nick" fighter plane. It first was reported as being tank-mounted on Saipan. Documentary evidence shows this weapon to be superior to the standard Type 94 (1934) 37-mm tank gun. It uses a cartridge case 6.53 inches long, and has a muzzle velocity of approximately 2,200 feet per second. It has the same gun and barrel length as the Type 94, suggesting that it is the same weapon rechambered to take the longer cartridge case.

CHARACTERISTICS:

Caliber	37 mm (1.46 inches).
Over-all length	53.9 inches.
Barrel length	49.5 inches.
Ammunition	AP and HE.

Type 1 (1941) 37-mm Tank Gun

This weapon is known to be the primary armament of the Type 2 (1942) amphibious tank. The weapon recovered was not in condition to be test fired, nor have any ammunition data been reported. Measurements of the chamber show conclusively that this weapon uses a cartridge case larger than that used with any other known Japanese 37-mm gun. A higher muzzle velocity than that of the Type 98 (1938) 37-mm tank gun is therefore indicated.

CHARACTERISTICS:

Caliber	37 mm (1.46 inches).
Length overall	67 inches.
Length of rifling	52.89 inches.
Length of chamber	10.0 inches.
Depth of breech recess	4.17 inches.

Type 1 (1941) 47-mm Tank Gun

This tank gun appears to be a modified version of the Type 1 (1941) 47-mm Japanese antitank gun. The sliding wedge breechblock, however, has been changed from the horizontal to a vertical position. It is a high-velocity gun, equipped with a hydrospring recoil mechanism and a semiautomatic breechblock. As the gun is mounted at the point of balance, no equilibrators are used.

Tests have shown that the gun will penetrate at least 3.25 inches of armor plate at 500 yards, at normal angle of impact.

CHARACTERISTICS:

Caliber	47 mm (1.85 inches).
Length over-all	88.75 inches.
Length of tube	84.75 inches.
Weight complete	906.25 pounds.
Weight of tube	361.62 pounds.
Weight of breechblock	34.62 pounds.
Weight of cradle assembly	366 pounds.
Ammunition	AP and HE.
Muzzle velocity	2,700 feet per second.

This gun is equipped with an excellent 4 x 14° panoramic telescopic sight, resembling the M6 sight used with the U. S. 37-mm antitank gun M3. The sight is equipped with a night lighting device, located at the front end, directly over the reticle lens.

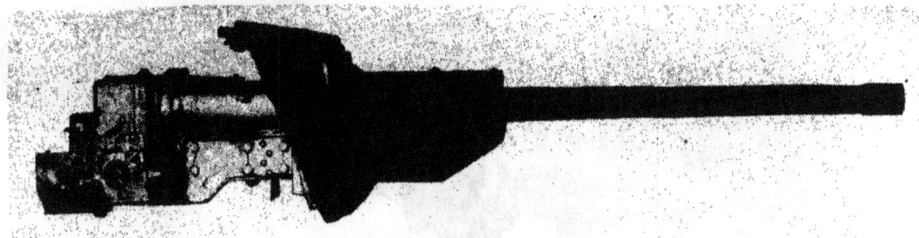

Figure 100.—Type 1 (1941) 47-mm tank gun.

Type 90 (1930) 57-mm Tank Gun

The Type 90 (1930) 57-mm tank gun appears to have been the forerunner of the Type 97 (1937) 57-mm tank gun. The Type 90 is a short-barreled weapon with a low muzzle velocity. The Japanese report that it is the primary armament of the Types 89A and 89B (1929) medium tanks. The tube of this weapon is of monobloc construction.

DOCUMENTARY CHARACTERISTICS:

Caliber	57 mm (2.24 inches).
Barrel length	41.2 inches.
Muzzle velocity	1,150 feet per second.
Range	5,900 yards at 30°.
Recoil mechanism	Hydrospring.
Weight of barrel with breech	135.5 pounds.*
Weight of cradle	103.6 pounds.*
Weight of mount	4.63 pounds.*
Ammunition	AP, HE, and HEAT.

*Questionable figures.

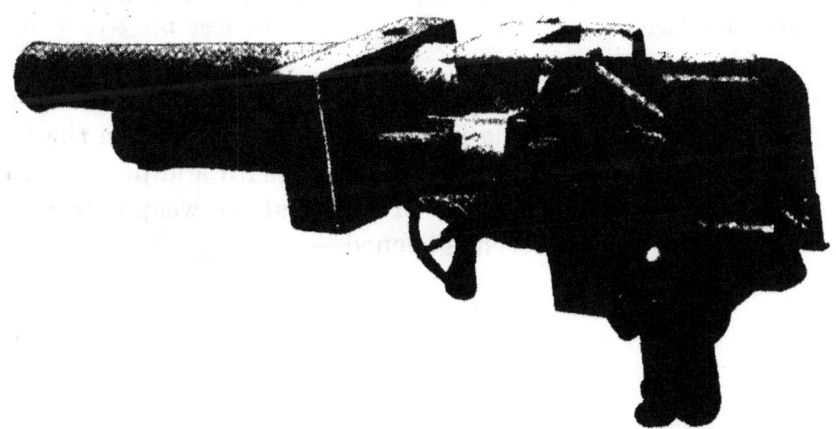

Figure 101.—Type 90 (1930) 57-mm tank gun, left side.

Figure 102.—Type 90 (1930) 57-mm tank gun, right side.

Type 97 (1937) 57-mm Tank Gun

Although several specimens of this gun have been captured, their condition prevented a detailed examination. Sufficient information is available, however, to indicate that this gun is a short-barreled, low-velocity weapon which probably is used in conjunction with a straight telescopic sight.

CHARACTERISTICS:

Caliber	57 mm (2.24 inches).
Weight of tube	283 pounds.
Length of tube	3 feet, 1.6 inches.
Length of chamber	5.1 inches.
Number of lands and grooves	20.
Recoil system	Hydrospring.
Maximum length of recoil	11 inches.
Type of breechblock	Vertical-sliding wedge.
Ammunition	AP, HE, and HEAT.
Armor penetration	0.79 inch with HEAT.
Muzzle velocity	1,260 feet per second (estimated).

The breech ring is box-shaped, and the breechblock is of the sliding, semiautomatic type. Firing is effected with a trigger on the left side of the gun which is protected by a trigger guard and pistol grip. The cocking lever is actuated by the breech, and the weapon is automatically cocked when the breech is opened.

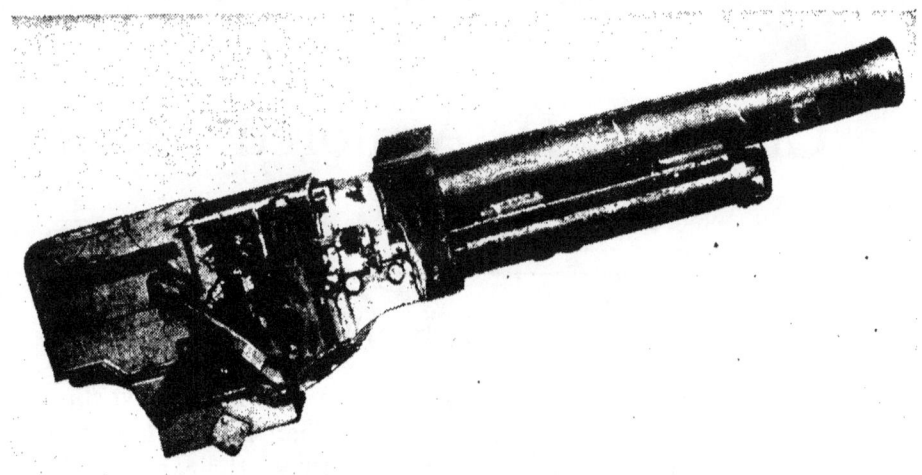

Figure 103.—Type 97 (1937) 57-mm tank gun. This gun is reported to be identical in external appearance with Type 90.

Type 94 (1934) 70-mm Tank Gun

This weapon is reported in documents, but has not as yet been recovered. The same cartridge case as that of the Type 92 70-mm infantry gun is used.

CHARACTERISTICS:

Caliber	70 mm (2.76 inches).
Weight	716 pounds.
Range	5,000 yards at 20 degrees elevation.
Tube length	50.6 inches.
Recoil system	Hydrospring.
Maximum recoil	11.8 inches.
Muzzle velocity:	
With AP	980 feet per second.
With HE	1,142 feet per second.
Ammunition	AP, HE, and HEAT.
Armor penetration	3.15 inches with HEAT; 0.98 inch with AP at 1,094 yards.

Type 99 (1939) 75-mm Tank Gun (Experimental)

Little is known of this weapon. It is referred to in documents as the new 75-mm gun which will be mounted as the primary armament in new Japanese medium tanks. It is probable that this weapon will have a performance considerably superior to any Japanese 75-mm gun encountered to date.

CHAPTER II. Armored Tactics

Introduction

The Japanese gave no real attention to mechanized warfare until after their disastrous experience with Russian armored units on the Manchurian border in 1939. Prior to 1939, their armored forces consisted of independent tank regiments and of tank groups comprising three or four tank regiments, a signal unit, and an engineer unit. After 1939, however, the Japanese apparently planned the creation of an armored army under an independent command. In pursuance of this new policy, two armored divisions were activated in 1942. An additional armored division was also activated in 1942, but not as a part of the armored army command.

In 1943, it is believed, the Japanese realized their inability to create the armored army as originally planned. This may have been primarily attributable to shipping difficulties and the higher manufacturing priorities of other items such as airplanes. The armored army accordingly was deactivated in November 1943, and its organic divisions were placed under new commands. Nevertheless another armored division was activated in 1944 subsequent to the deactivation of the armored army.

Organization of Armored Units

Available information indicates that the original armored divisions were organized as square (brigaded) divisions. These divisions were triangularized in early 1944, however, and the new division activated that year was triangular. Estimated table-of-organization strength of such a triangular armored division is 12,950 officers and men, 175 medium tanks, and 141 light tanks. But armored divisions, like all Japanese units, deviate from the established table of organization. Thus far, two divisions have been encountered in combat without either their antiaircraft defense units or their reconnaissance units.

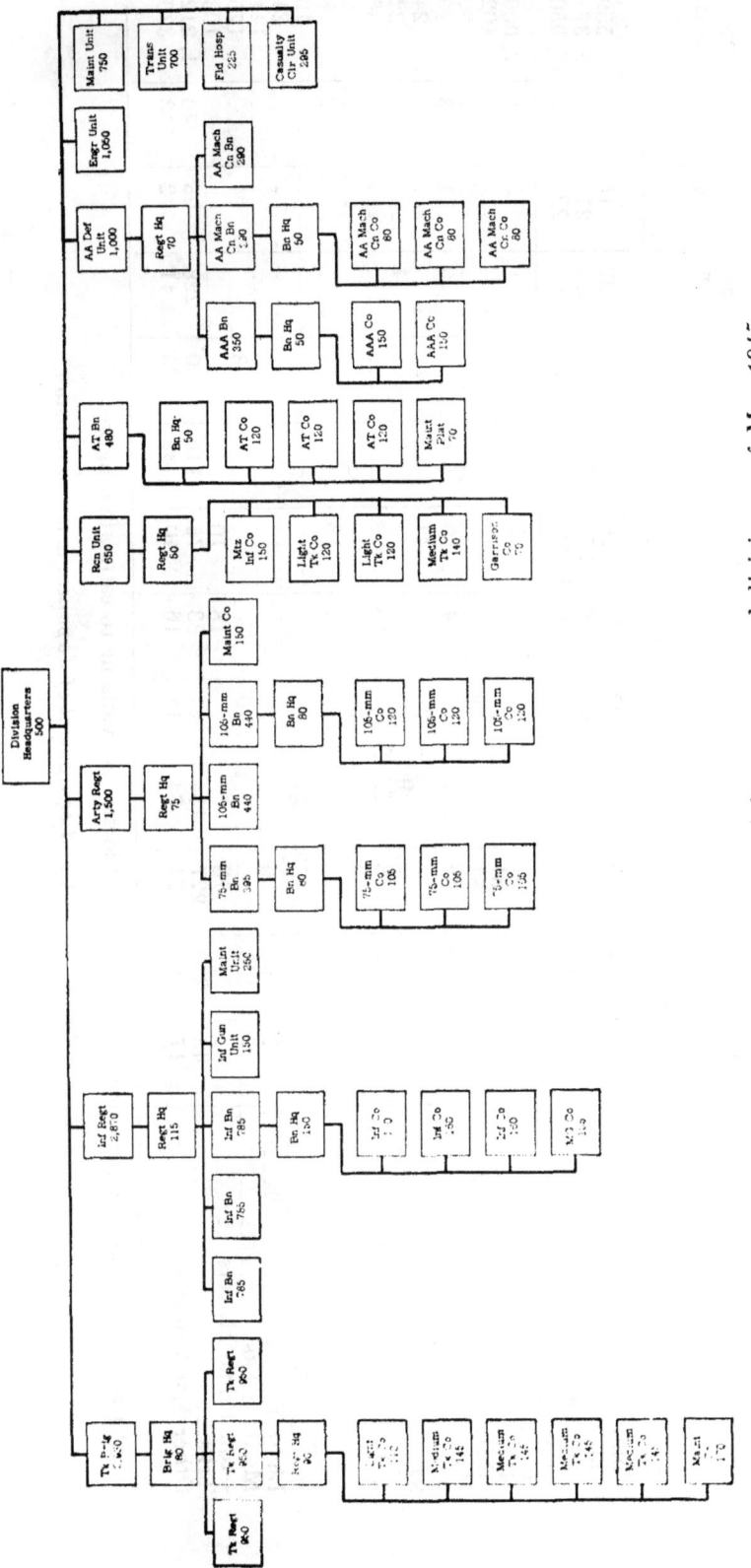

Figure 104.—Table of organization of Japanese armored division as of May 1945.

Strength and Equipment	Div Hq	Tk Brig	Inf Regt	Arty Regt	Rcn Unit	AT Bn	AA Def Unit	Engr Unit	Maint Unit	Trans Unit	Fld Hosp	Casualty Clr Unit	Div Total
Commissioned	60	137	95	85	23	24	30	39	20	22	15	9	559
Enlisted	440	2,793	2,775	1,415	627	456	970	1,011	730	678	210	286	12,391
Aggregate	500	2,930	2,870	1,500	650	480	1,000	1,050	750	700	225	295	12,950
Rs	( )[1]	( )	( )	( )	( )	( )	( )	( )	( )	( )	( )	( )	7,000
GDs			81		9			12					102
LMGs			81		9								90
Hv MGs		9	39			4		6		8	1	3	70
20-mm AA Mach Guns							24						24
37-mm AT Guns			18	9	3			6		4			22
47-mm AT Guns			6			18							36
75-mm Regtl Guns													6
75-mm AA Guns							8						8
105-mm Hows				12									12
Light Tks	2	95	9	24	32				3				141
Medium Tks	7	155			10				3				175
4-ton Prime Movers				57			10						103
Trks	43	200	227	134	41	33	75	116	50	228	25	40	1,212
Other Mtr Vehicles	17	40	74	64	11	16	40	37	25	41	2	3	370

[1] Parentheses indicate presence but insufficient evidence is available to estimate a figure.

Figure 105.—Strength and equipment of Japanese armored division.

Strength and Equipment	Brig Hq	Tk Regt					Brig Total 3 Tk Regts
		Regtl Hq	Medium Tk Co	Light Tk Co	Maint Co	Regtl Total 1 Light Tk Co 4 Medium Tk Cos 1 Maint Co	
Commissioned	8	12	5	5	6	43	137
Enlisted	72	78	140	105	164	907	2,793
Aggregate	80	90	145	110	170	950	2,930
Rs	( )[1]	( )	( )	( )	( )	( )	( )
Hv MGs					3	3	9
Light Tks	2	3	4	12		31	95
Medium Tks	5	4	11		2	50	155
Trks	8	6	5	4	34	64	200
Other Mtr Vehicles	4	4	1	1	3	12	40

[1] Parentheses indicate presence but insufficient evidence is available to estimate a figure.

Figure 106.—Strength and equipment of Japanese tank brigade (armored division).

Strength and Equipment	Regtl Hq	Bn				Inf Gun Unit	Maint Unit	Regt Total 3 Bns 1 Inf Gun Unit 1 Maint Co
		Bn Hq	Co	MG Co	Bn Total 3 Cos 1 MG Co			
Commissioned	9	8	4	4	24	5	9	95
Enlisted	106	142	156	151	761	145	241	2,775
Total	115	150	160	155	785	150	250	2,870
Rs	( )[1]	( )	( )	( )	( )	( )	( )	( )
GDs			9		27			81
LMGs			9		27			81
Hv MGs				12	12		3	39
47-mm AT Guns			2		6			18
75-mm Regtl Guns						6		6
Light Tks		3			3			9
4-ton Prime Movers			2		6			18
Trks	12	12	11	11	56	12	35	227
Other Mtr Vehicles	4	8	2	2	16	2	20	74

[1] Parentheses indicate presence but insufficient evidence is available to estimate a figure.

Figure 107.—Strength and equipment of Japanese infantry regiment (armored division).

Strength and Equipment	Regtl Hq	75-mm Bn			105-mm Bn			Maint Co	Regtl Total 1 75-mm Bn 2 105-mm Bns 1 Maint Co
		Bn Hq	Co	Bn Total 3 cos	Bn Hq	Co	Bn Total 3 cos		
Commissioned	11	10	4	22	11	4	23	6	85
Enlisted	64	70	101	373	69	116	417	144	1,415
Aggregate	75	80	105	395	80	120	440	150	1,500
Rs	( )¹	( )	( )	( )	( )	( )	( )	( )	( )
37-mm AT Guns			1	3		1	3		9
75-mm Guns			4	12					12
105-mm Hows						4	12		12
4-ton Prime Movers			9	27		5	15		57
Trks	4	5	6	23	5	10	35	37	134
Other Mtr Vehicles	7	6	3	15	6	3	15	12	64

¹ Parentheses indicate presence but insufficient evidence to estimate a figure.

Figure 108. Strength and equipment of Japanese artillery regiment (armored division).

In addition to the armored units included in the triangular armored divisions, the Japanese have several types of independent units. There were originally nearly 20 independent tank regiments. Of these, one was rendered ineffective in the Marianas in July 1944, and one was absorbed by independent mixed regiments on Marcus and Wake. The remaining regiments still operate independently. The table-of-organization strength of the independent tank regiment is approximately 950 officers and men, 31 light tanks, and 50 medium tanks.

The Japanese also have independent tank companies with a table-of-organization strength of approximately 150 officers and men, ten medium tanks, and two light tanks. Originally, 11 of these tank companies were known to exist; two of these were rendered ineffective on Saipan.

Four independent tankette companies are known to be in existence at present. These companies have a table-of-organization strength of 130 officers and men, and 17 tankettes.

In 1942, several infantry divisions had either tank units (strength 750) or infantry group tankette companies (strength 100), and sometimes both types of organization. Most of these units were demobilized by early 1944. At the present time, only four infantry divisions are known to have tank units. A recently observed trend, however, has been to have two armored-car or light-tank companies in the division reconnaissance regiments. Such a disposition would make eight to twelve light tanks available to the infantry division.

Japanese Armored Tactical Principles

Basic Doctrine

The Japanese battle principles and concepts presented here are based upon present doctrine and teaching, and on the very limited use of armor encountered up to the present time. It cannot be emphasized too strongly that Japanese tank operations to date have consisted of piecemeal tank counterattacks and defensive siting of tanks as pillboxes in direct contradiction to promulgated doctrine.

Missions

Japanese Field Service Regulations definitely stress the point that all arms must be used to enable the infantry to close with the enemy and annihilate him. This indicates that the basic mission of tanks is still believed to be direct cooperation with infantry.

Present Japanese teachings describe the principal function of the tank to be "to pave the way for a victory for the entire army by bringing into full play their great mobility and striking force; by containing and destroying the enemy fighting power in detail after making penetrations into the hostile lines; and by expediting prompt exploitation through the coordinated efforts of the participating units."

Similarly, the mission of tanks is prescribed to be "closely to support infantry (cavalry) combat. Depending on the situation, they will infiltrate into the hostile area in order to seize the initiative or to seal the enemy's fate. In the mechanized unit, of which the tank is the main element, they become the very core of a tremendous striking force."

Formations

According to the *Japanese Field Service Regulations*, the platoon deploys normally in a diamond formation, and the company in a diamond of diamonds. The normal combat formation is a "T." The company is disposed with three platoons abreast and one platoon trailing. Each platoon is in a diamond formation.

Although no large formations of Japanese tanks have been encountered, the Japanese Army Tank School gives precise instructions for the employment of such formations. For an attack on a lightly held enemy position, Japanese doctrine specifies a minimum of 30 to 40 tanks. If the enemy is in a strongly defended position, at least 60 tanks are required. If hostile artillery shelling and aerial bombing are unusually heavy, 100 tanks are necessary.

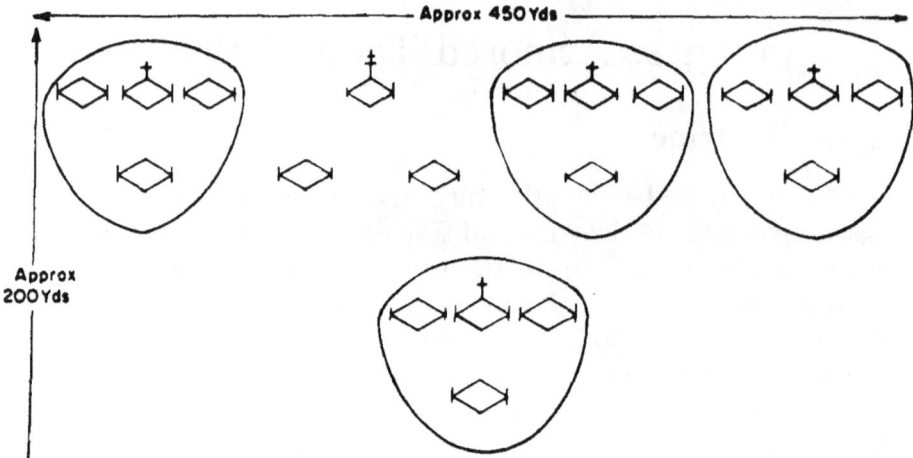

Figure 109.—Japanese tank platoon and tank company in deployed formations.

Japanese tactical doctrine stresses the use of tanks in what is called a "mobile mass." When committed in this manner, tanks constitute the main fire element in what is essentially an attempt to attain a decisive victory by one stroke, preferably by attacking a weak spot in the hostile line. Since the nature of the terrain is considered to be the chief limitation on the employment of large tank formations, such tactics are to be resorted to only in suitable terrain. In any case, tanks are committed as a "mobile mass" only at "a momentous time and place, when a decision of the entire army is in balance."

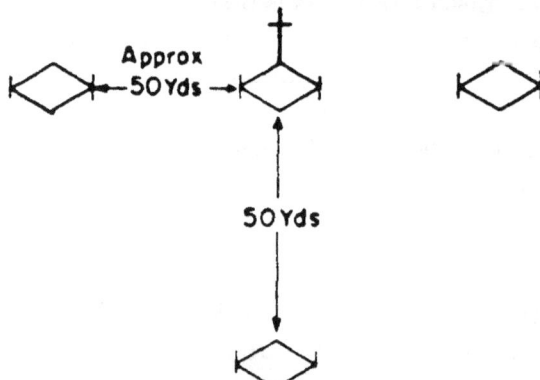

Figure 110.—T-formation.

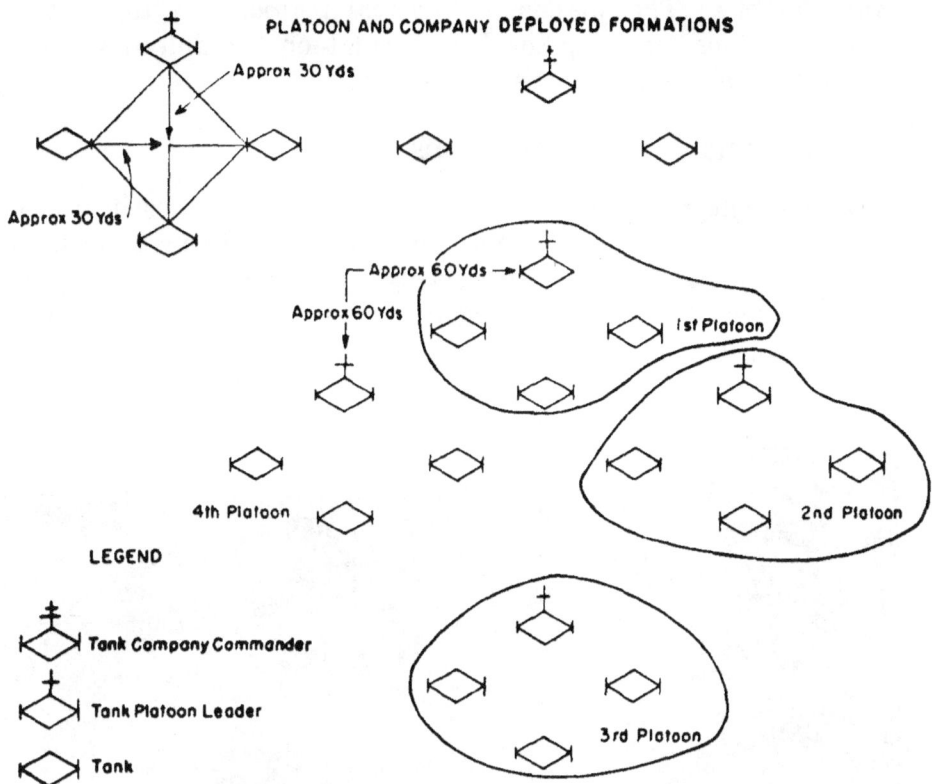

Figure 111.—Japanese tank company formations.

Japanese tanks, when employed as a "mobile mass," are allocated into two echelons, in keeping with combat principles for the company and regiment. Dispositions of tanks within the company and regiment are made by the company and regimental commander, respectively.

Deployment in Two Lines

Japanese Field Service Regulations further prescribe that "the regiment will usually deploy its entire strength along the front line, but, as the situation demands, tanks are disposed in two lines." When deployed in two lines, the missions of the second line is to liquidate the enemy surviving the assault of the first line, or to liquidate hostile antitank weapons. If the situation warrants, the second line will execute an enveloping attack against the enemy, or attempt a "passage of lines" through the first line to carry on the attack. At times, the first and second lines will launch simultaneous attacks to neutralize the enemy line in depth completely.

A Japanese tank company ordinarily is deployed into two lines of tank platoons. The missions of the rear platoons are to attack the enemy weapons surviving the forward platoons' assault and to attack the hostile antitank weapons.

Deployment in Two Echelons

When a tank group or larger unit is directed against hostile positions in depth, the attacking tanks may be formed into two echelons. The reserve echelon of a large unit ordinarily is held to meet any emergency, or it may be set up to exploit such success that may be won by the forward echelons.

Figure 112.—Type 94 (1934) medium tanks deployed in China.

Tanks in Infantry Support

Two Types of Cooperation

Despite the doctrine of mass employment, no large Japanese tank forces have been encountered, and the infantry support role has been exclusively emphasized. In general there are two Japanese methods of infantry-tank cooperation. One requires the tank commander to designate the infantry forces with which the tanks are to cooperate, in response to requests for support received from the infantry commanders. The other method is predicated upon advance specification of the objectives for the tanks' attacks.

When the tanks are allotted directly to infantry units, the tank regimental commander gives the general outline of the plan of action, leaving the details of execution to the tank company commanders.

For example, if it is necessary for the tanks to execute a reversal of movement to facilitate the forward advance of the infantry, the movement is made on order of the tank company commanders, often in response to a direct request from the infantry for the maneuver.

On the other hand, if tanks are assigned specific objectives, the tank regiment commander retains direct control throughout the entire course of the action, and the tanks are committed as a unit. This method of tank-infantry cooperation is favored when time is short and it is difficult to foresee changes in the situation that may ensue during the action. It should be noted that in this method of cooperation the tanks may be committed by platoons. When tanks are assigned to infantry units, however, nothing less than a tank company is committed.

Exploitation Operations

In exploitation operations, Japanese tanks are committed to seize tactically important areas, confuse hostile attack deployments, and strike at enemy artillery or other vital rear installations. If tanks are to give impetus and momentum to the infantry assault, they advance in close coordination with the infantry. It is always possible, according to Japanese doctrine, to employ both methods simultaneously, especially if an ample number of tanks is available. Some can be used in direct support missions, while the remainder are held in reserve to exploit successes achieved by the assault wave. If more tanks are available than the estimated requirements for close infantry support, some may be committed as leading tanks, usually under division control.

Principles of Infantry-Tank Attacks

A number of fundamental principles are emphasized in Japanese infantry-tank attack doctrine. Close liaison is maintained at all times. Liaison means include radio, joint command posts, liaison officers, visual signaling, and tank runners. Until recently, available information indicated that only the platoon commander's tank was equipped with a radio. In the 2nd Armored Division on Luzon, however, it was found that all medium tanks and practically all light tanks encountered were equipped with well-built, two-way radios.

When tanks are used as runners, two tanks are used for each assignment. If necessary, tanks are rallied frequently to insure maximum coordination of offensive action. If the infantry assault fails to progress as planned, the tanks concentrate on those enemy obstacles or strongpoints constituting the most effective impediments to the infantry advance. Prompt and vigorous action is taken against enemy positions delivering flanking fire on the Japanese infantry.

If Japanese tanks encounter an antitank installation within the enemy position, Japanese doctrine prescribes that an immediate decision must be made whether to bypass the installation or to liquidate it by frontal assault. Incipient enemy counterattacks are frustrated by striking at the counterattack base, the infantry deployed for the counterattack, or the hostile tanks which may be spearheading the maneuver, depending upon the situation.

Areas are designated for rallying of the tanks after the accomplishment of their mission and preparing for the next phase. Tanks also assemble at rally points when the assault is suspended at night or broken off because of the tenacity of enemy resistance. Restoration of combat strength is the principal object of rallying. With this in mind, the Japanese choose sites to afford the maximum efficiency in regroupment, replacement, and repair. Special care is taken to collect all damaged vehicles and to initiate repair when feasible.

Engineer Parties

Tank attacks or infantry attacks supported by tanks sometimes are facilitated by the assignment of engineer parties to cooperate with the tanks. Personnel of these parties are especially trained in the techniques of demolishing tank traps and other obstacles that might impede the advance of tanks or a tank-supported infantry attack.

In one observed instance, the engineer party consisted of a leader and five men equipped with 122 pounds of explosive, a smoke discharger, picks, shovels, and other tools. Both personnel and equipment were carried on the outside of two tanks. The tanks stopped about 10 yards from an obstacle to permit the men to dismount and unload. The tanks then withdrew to a position about 50 yards to the rear and covered the demolition operations by tank-gun and machine-gun fire. The Japanese anticipate the prompt demolition of obstacles by this method.

Orders for the Attack

The Japanese stress the issuance of precise orders that clearly specify objectives in actions involving infantry-tank cooperation. When tanks are attached to an infantry battalion, they are under the control of the infantry commander. Company commanders are expected, however, to maintain liaison with the tank commander to facilitate cooperation and expedite prompt exploitation of tank successes by the infantry.

The infantry battalion commander's orders to the tank unit commander include a statement of the general plan. Tank objectives are clearly specified, and the obstacles to be removed are designated. Assembly areas, line of departure, H-hour, and the methods to be used by the tanks in crossing the line of their infantry are prescribed. It should be noted that Japanese doctrine does not provide for the assignment of phase lines, bomb lines, or boundaries between units below divisions, although a few instances have been noted in which regimental boundaries were prescribed.

Infantry company commanders are expected to keep the battalion commander informed of the nature and location of primary tank objectives in their sectors to enable the battalion commander to assign precise objectives.

Use of Tanks Against Hostile Flanks

In the event that there are no primary tank objectives requiring immediate action, or their location cannot be ascertained, the tanks may be employed against the enemy's flanks. When employed in flank attacks, the battalion commander theoretically sends infantry with the tanks for a coordinated assault. The infantry is also given the mission of mopping up pockets of resistance which survive the initial assault. Infantry units assigned these missions usually are taken from front-line companies opposite the flank or flanks subject to the attack.

Japanese tactical doctrine for a flank attack directs the infantry battalion commander to concentrate his fire power against the enemy antitank weapons. If necessary, details are sent forward to clear lanes for the passage of tanks through areas containing antitank weapons or where antitank weapons can be expected. Japanese doctrine also emphasizes the necessity for infantry to cover and protect the tanks from antitank fire. Despite the promulgation of this doctrine, unaccompanied Japanese tanks were sent against U. S. antitank weapons on Guadalcanal and were completely annihilated.

Tank Regiment Tactics

During an advance, the frontage of a tank regiment will be 500 to 550 yards. The advance is preceded by a patrol of tankettes for reconnaissance, followed by a "direct guard" (advance guard), consisting of a light tank platoon to develop enemy positions prior to the assault. Regimental headquarters follows the "direct guard" and is in turn followed by a forward platoon of light or medium tanks to deal with enemy antitank weapons that open fire. Then comes the main body, consisting of the remainder of the company furnishing the "direct guard" and forward platoons, flanked on either side by a tank company. The fourth company, in a four-company regiment, brings up the rear. A medium tank company on the march, according to logistical data, will form a column 915 yards long; a light company, one of 526 yards.

If the estimated depth of the enemy position is about 1,500 yards, the Japanese assume it will be defended by at least two or three antitank guns, six heavy machine guns, five mortars, and nine to twelve light machine guns. The frontage of a Japanese regiment in an attack on such a position will be 550 to 875 yards, and a tank company will be assigned to the support of each infantry battalion.

The attack is made in three echelons. The first, under the direct control of the tank regimental commander, has as its objective the establishment of a passage for the infantry. The tanks of this echelon neutralize the enemy antitank guns and strongpoints not destroyed by the artillery preparation. Those positions not liquidated by the initial attack are subsequently mopped up by the infantry. This procedure differs from a small-scale employment of tanks in support of infantry, in which case Japanese doctrine assigns the liquidation of enemy antitank weapons to the infantry instead of the first tank echelon.

The second tank echelon, under the direct control of the infantry battalion commander in charge of the infantry assault wave, leads and supports the infantry by pinning down or liquidating enemy automatic-weapons personnel.

The third tank echelon, under regimental control, is held in reserve to exploit successes of the first two echelons. If a breakthrough is made by the first echelons, the reserve is committed to strike, as deeply as possible, in the enemy's rear areas.

Tank Division Tactics

Japanese doctrine states that the front of a division in an attack will be about 2,735 yards. When an armored division is attached to an infantry division, the tanks are committed in three echelons. Two infantry regiments are in the front line, each preceded from 400 to 500 yards by a tank company. The primary mission of the first tank echelon is to neutralize enemy antitank weapons and strongpoints not destroyed by artillery fire, and to clear a path for the second echelon composed of the major infantry assault units and their assigned tanks.

The second tank echelon is deployed immediately in front of the major infantry assault units (two infantry regiments), with one company in front of each of the four battalions. The mission of the tanks in this echelon is to cover and support the infantry assault with special attention to liquidating enemy automatic weapons. When warranted, these tanks may leapfrog through the first echelon.

A regiment of tanks, comprising the third echelon, is held in reserve under the direct control of the division commander. The mission of the third echelon is to exploit the success of the assault; it may also be used to reinforce any area requiring aid, perhaps by attachment to an infantry unit.

Tanks in Close-Support Roles

When the tank support for the infantry must be exceptionally close, some important modifications in Japanese tactics are made, including organization of the tank regiment into two combat units. The first combat unit is divided into a left and right formation, each of which is preceded by a patrol of light tanks to develop the enemy position and draw enemy antitank fire. Both of the formations consist of four platoons arranged into two columns of two platoons each. The two front platoons advance with the infantry; the two rear platoons are used to swing around the flanks of the leading platoons to engage located enemy antitank weapons. Each of the two formations is followed by a platoon of engineers.

The second combat unit consists of four platoons. One platoon is assigned the mission of neutralizing antitank guns and self-propelled artillery. The remaining three platoons are assigned the mission of liquidating automatic weapons. One of them may be used as a reserve or to exploit successes. The regimental headquarters moves with this combat unit following the first platoon.

Example of Tank Division Tactics

The 2nd Armored Division on Luzon was the first unit encountered by U. S. forces. It was anticipated that the commitment of this Japanese armored force would provide valuable material for a study of Japanese methods in the employment of massed armor and coordinated infantry-armor-artillery tactics. Actual operations, however, revealed that the Japanese commanders either did not understand the modern concept of armor employment or simply were unable to employ the armored division in accordance with promulgated principles of operation. Instead, the Japanese commanders frittered away the division in piecemeal counterattacks and immobile defenses. They never mounted an attack with more than 16 tanks at one time. The principle of mass was never employed. The inherent mobility of the tanks was not utilized, but was negated by committing the tanks to fixed defensive emplacements.

The greatest concentrations of Japanese tanks were in San Manuel and Munoz. Here, the armor, committed to a death stand, was dug in so that only the turrets were exposed. Emplacements had heavy adobe revetments, were under heavy foliage, and were a nucleus for all other defensive measures. Tanks were sited to cover the highways and cross-country approaches with mutually supporting fires. Close-in security of the armored pillboxes was provided by automatic weapons and infantry dug in around each tank. Artillery, emplaced in covered positions, supplemented the tanks to complete an integrated fire plan. Last-resort counterattacks were launched at night once the local defenses were doomed.

Infantry-Artillery-Tank Coordination

Japanese doctrine prescribes that when artillery and tanks cooperate with the infantry, support must be carefully coordinated. When the infantry attacks immediately after the artillery preparation, the tanks should have a line of departure and jump-off time that will not interfere with the consummation of the artillery plan or the full realization of its potentialities by the infantry. The danger of friendly artillery fire is to be disregarded when it is necessary for the tanks to neutralize unexpected enemy flanking capabilities. In the absence of artillery preparation, the tanks ordinarily initiate their attack immediately upon completion of the infantry's preparatory phase.

Special Tank Operations

Dawn Attacks

A dawn attack is really a night maneuver for Japanese tanks. Tanks normally are directed to proceed to the line of departure under cover of darkness guided by noncommissioned officers especially trained in tank tactics. Thorough preparation is made with emphasis on the removal of natural and artificial obstacles to the advance of the tanks, or provision to bypass such obstacles. The exact procedure to be followed by the tanks in leapfrogging the infantry preparatory to spearheading the attack is prescribed well in advance.

Night Attacks

Preparations for night attacks are even more elaborate and precise than for dawn attacks. As much as a platoon of tanks may be assigned to one infantry company. Tank objectives include heavy weapons of the enemy's first line of defense, obstacles, and flank defenses. Objectives are designated preferably to permit the tanks to move to the line of departure in daylight unless enemy observation renders such movement impracticable.

Pursuit

The Japanese feel that pursuit affords the best opportunity for exploiting the advantages of the tanks to the maximum. It is considered necessary to plan maintenance and supply facilities to preserve the continuity of the pursuit. Clear objectives are selected, and the tanks are ordered to proceed against them as directly as possible regardless of losses. Pursuit, the Japanese say, should be unremitting and audacious, even if only one tank survives to complete the mission.

Tank-Versus-Tank Action

Tank operations theoretically are not conducted with the purpose of precipitating tank-versus-tank engagements. Despite this theory, Japanese tank commanders, when confronted by a modern well-equipped army, have been directed to be in a constant state of readiness to engage enemy tanks.

In tank-versus-tank engagements the Japanese believe that the retention of the initiative is the prerequisite for success. Foresight, quick commands, firm determination, and cohesive organization are the attributes described as necessary for the retention of the initiative. Tank units are expected to proceed on the assumption that they enjoy superiority in situations requiring quick decisions and are directed to launch immediate attacks against the flanks and rear of enemy tank formations. Japanese armor will fight in closely integrated and controlled maneuvers, attempting to defeat the enemy tanks in detail. Japanese doctrine prescribes the concentration of fire on enemy command and leading tanks.

Long-Range Raids

Long-range raids leading to meeting engagements receive considerable attention in Japanese doctrine. In such an operation, advance on a 325- to 550-yard front is prescribed. A reconnaissance unit is the advance force with the mission of obtaining all possible information on the terrain, routes of advance, enemy forces and their dispositions, and other intelligence of possible use to the commander of the advancing tank regiment. An advance guard, consisting of one tank platoon, with the mission of driving-in light enemy resistance encountered, or of developing resistance, follows the reconnaissance unit. Regimental headquarters follows the advance guard and is in turn followed by a tank company advancing on a 55- to 120-yard front. The field artillery attached to the tank regiment and the engineer unit follow in parallel columns behind the first tank company. A tank company is abreast of and parallel to the artillery and engineer columns on each flank. These flank tank companies are used for enveloping maneuvers or to assist the leading tank company in the destruction of enemy obstacles and antitank weapons. The artillery is used in a direct-support role, and the engineers assist in the reduction of obstacles. Behind the artillery and engineers with their flank tank companies, is the infantry, which is usually motorized. The infantry may be used for a frontal assault or for a holding attack coordinated with an enveloping maneuver. The infantry is followed by a second echelon of tanks as a reserve. The reserve, committed as the situation warrants, can be used to exploit penetrations or to reinforce other tank units.

Raids

In contrast to the long-range raids by at least a regiment, similar Japanese tank units are used on so-called raids. Raids are undertaken often upon the request of infantry commanders, to capture critical terrain features, confuse the enemy, or to deliver surprise strikes on artillery, headquarters, or other important installations. Since heavy losses are expected, such raids are undertaken only when the anticipated results will justify the loss. The frontage used is from 650 to 765 yards, and the depth of the formation is from 440 to 660 yards. The tanks are divided into two combat units. The first combat unit is assigned the mission of liquidating enemy antitank weapons, while the second combat unit is assigned the mission of destroying or neutralizing hostile automatic weapons.

Tanks in Defense

Japanese defense doctrine emphasizes the offensive almost exclusively. The defense is considered to be a temporary phase of combat which the Japanese must accept because of overwhelming enemy superiority. The object of the defense is to deplete the enemy's strength until a counterattack can be initiated. The Japanese views on defensive combat, coupled with the predominantly offensive character of the tank, cause a lack of attention to defensive tactics. Japanese doctrine prescribes the use of tanks in counterattacks. They are expected to deliver short, speedy assaults upon the objectives in close cooperation with artillery. The engagement is to be broken off upon completion of the mission. If enemy tanks are present in superior numbers, counterattacking Japanese tanks try to coordinate their action with their own antitank-weapons fire. In recent operations, the Japanese dug in their tanks and used them defensively as artillery and antitank weapons.

Summary

A comparison of Japanese doctrine with actual operations to date definitely reveals a complete failure on the part of Japanese commanders to employ armored forces as prescribed by *Japanese Field Service Regulations*. Massed armor has never been used in offensive action. Defensive combat has been confined to a static defense with a final uncoordinated "banzai" counterattack. A truly coordinated attack has never materialized. The use of piecemeal, uncoordinated attacks may be due to physical impossibilities, lack of the proper means, a failure to understand the methods, or lack of training. In any event, one fact is paramount; to date the Japanese have not employed armor according to modern concepts.

CHAPTER III. Antitank Artillery

General Estimate

The Japanese are known to have only one artillery piece which they designate specifically as an antitank gun: the Type 1 (1941) 47-mm antitank gun. However, every artillery piece they possess, irrespective of size or caliber, is a potential antitank weapon, despite the fact that each piece is handicapped in the antitank role by specific design features. The principal handicap, which applies generally, is the lack of direct-fire sights for Japanese field guns. The Japanese panoramic telescope, set at zero, can be used in direct fire against moving targets, but this method cannot be as satisfactory as sights specifically designed for direct fire, such as elbow telescopes.

Mobility is an important characteristic of effective antitank guns which must displace frequently and rapidly. In this respect, driven spades have been reported to interfere with the mobility of the Japanese infantry guns and field artillery. This is true of the Type 1 (1941) 47-mm gun and Type 94 (1934) 37-mm gun as well as of all the late field artillery pieces.

The effectiveness of most Japanese field artillery pieces in an antitank role is further restricted by the lack of high muzzle velocities needed to develop sufficient hitting power to penetrate modern armor. Only one 75-mm piece, the Type 90, has a muzzle velocity greater than 2,000 feet per second.

Higher muzzle velocities are a feature of Japanese antiaircraft guns. Use of these guns in an antitank role, however, is restricted by their lack of mobility. Nevertheless, the Type 88 (1928) 75-mm antiaircraft gun has been used against ground targets, including tanks, and other heavy antiaircraft guns could be similarly employed. The Navy Type 96 (1936) 25-mm gun, with a muzzle velocity of 2,850 feet per second and firing a 10-ounce armor-piercing projectile, is effective against light tanks and the most vulnerable points of medium tanks.

This gun is frequently sited on beaches for direct fire against landing craft.

Japanese light and medium coast defense guns are suited to antitank roles, since they are equipped with on-carriage fire control for direct laying on moving targets, using telescopes. These guns are capable of causing considerable damage to Allied armor during landing operations. At one time the Japanese emplaced coast defense guns in open pits allowing a wide traverse; they now tend to sacrifice field of fire for concealment, and place coast defense weapons in cover.

Figure 113.—Typical Japanese coast defense gun position as currently employed.

It is now evident that the Japanese are endeavoring to improve the armor-piercing performance of their artillery weapons by the introduction of improved armor-piercing projectiles. The Type 1 (1941) APHE projectile is issued for various artillery weapons up through 150-mm pieces. The projectile generally is shorter and contains less high explosive than other APHE rounds.

In addition, the Japanese comparatively recently have introduced hollow-charge projectiles for their-low-muzzle velocity weapons. The Japanese claim that their hollow-charge projectile has an armor penetration approximately equal to the caliber of the weapon from which it is fired, but Allied trials have proved this to be an under-estimation. The following penetration figures are for Type 2 hollow charge.

ARMOR PENETRATION:

Gun	Penetration (inches)
Type 92 (1932) 70-mm howitzer	3.1
Type 41 (1908) 75-mm mountain (infantry) gun	3.3
Type 94 (1934) 75-mm mountain gun	3.3

Infantry Weapons

Critical Appraisal

Antitank weapons with which the Japanese Army has equipped its infantry units are for the most part inadequate against present-day armor. To date, neither antitank rocket launchers nor hollow-charge projectors have been encountered in the hands of the Japanese. They have made some effort to develop effective antitank rifle grenades. But so far the only effective antitank weapon furnished the Japanese infantry has been the Type 1 (1941) 47-mm gun. The Type 97 20-mm rifle, originally designed in 1937 for use against tanks, cannot be considered effective against modern armor. This weapon can be carried into positions inaccessible to other antitank weapons. It is, however, useless in tracking a moving target because the rear monopod must be pulled out of the ground and reset. The Type 11 (1922) 37-mm gun is now obsolete. It has been replaced by the Type 94 (1934) 37-mm gun. The Type 94 (1937) 37-mm gun was copied from a German design. It has knee-action shock absorbers and pneumatic tires for high-speed mobility.

The 5-cm (47-mm) short-barreled naval gun was copied from an obsolete British naval gun and intended by the Japanese for a Special Naval Landing Force gun. The only ammunition found for the gun so far is an armor-piercing projectile with corrugated copper rotating bands. Because of the weak powder charge of the ammunition, the short barrel (4 feet, 8 inches), and the fact that the gun cannot be freely traversed, it would be of little value as an antitank weapon.

Neither the Type 92 (1932) 70-mm battalion howitzer nor the Type 41 (1908) 75-mm mountain (infantry) gun can be considered effective in an antitank role, although hollow-charge and APHE ammunition for the 75-mm weapon is available.

Only the Type 1 47-mm gun has adequate fire control equipment for an antitank role. The 37-mm weapons are fitted with straight telescopes. The 70-mm battalion howitzer sight is a panoramic 3-power telescope mounted on the left, above the breech. To lay the gun for direct fire, one man must sight through the telescope and turn the elevating and traversing handwheels until the cross hairs are on the target. Leads must be estimated without the aid of a mil-scale reticle. The same sight, Type 95B, is fitted on the Type 41 75-mm gun. Difficulties of firing at tanks with both the Type 92 and Type 41 are increased by the fact that traversing and elevating handwheels are on opposite sides of the carriage, while only one telescope is provided.

Type 94 (1934) 37-mm Gun

This weapon is distributed widely throughout the Japanese Army. It is the organic weapon of infantry units and is also issued to independent antitank and armored units, although the appearance of the Type 1 (1941) 47-mm gun has made the Type 94 37-mm weapon a substitute standard gun in the antitank role. However, the 37-mm gun has proved to be an effective infantry close-support weapon. The Japanese fire it against tanks and armored cars, loopholes of embrasures, and automatic weapons. Light and easily handled, the Type 94 can be emplaced for action very quickly. Since the gun is only 3 feet, 4½ inches high it can be easily concealed.

The tube is of monobloc construction with the slipper integral with the barrel. It has a semiautomatic, horizontal sliding breechblock which opens on recoil and ejects the empty cartridge case. The breech is retained in the open position by the extractors. When another round is loaded, the extractors are released and the breech, powered by a spring, closes.

The gun is laid in elevation by two distinct and independent elevating mechanisms. One is the small handwheel on the left which contains the firing knob. It moves the straight telescope and the barrel. Thus, for direct firing one man can control the aiming, elevating, and traversing mechanisms. He fires the gun by pulling the knob on the elevating handwheel. The other elevation control is the large handwheel on the right which moves the barrel only. This handwheel operates the range drum, which has three scales. The left scale is graduated from 0 to 30 and is marked for armor-piercing shells. The center scale is graduated from 0 to 40, and is marked for high-explosive shells. The right scale is graduated from 0 to 50 and is marked for shrapnel.

The piece may be found mounted on wooden artillery wheels with steel tires, or on perforated steel disc wheels. In firing position, spades are driven in the ground at the end of the split trails. Spade brackets enable the spades to be locked in three positions; two for firing (hard or soft ground), and one for traveling. In action, the left-side stub axle is pivoted in its mounting, allowing the left wheel to be turned 45 degrees outward at the rear. This permits right traverse of the piece

Figure 114.—Type 94 (1934) 37-mm gun, steel-wheel version. Note driven spades.

without fouling the wheel. A spring-loaded locking arm locks the stub axle in either its normal or pivoted position.

For transportation, the weapon may be broken down into four sections and packed on horses or drawn by a single horse. The gun may also be man-carried, thus greatly increasing its tactical mobility.

SPECIFICATIONS:

Caliber	37 mm (1.45 inches).
Weight firing	720 pounds.
Length of tube	66.4 inches.
Traverse	60°.
Elevation	−10° to + 27°.
Muzzle velocity	2,327 feet per second.
Sight	Straight telescope.

AMMUNITION:

Fixed ammunition is used with the Type 94. A small cannelure behind the rotating band allows the cartridge case to be crimped to the projectile.

Projectile	Fuze	Weight (pounds)	Weight of Complete Round (pounds)
Type 94 AP	Type 94 short delay	1.54	2.9
Type 94 HE	Type 93 instantaneous	1.4	2.54
Type 13 HE	Type 14 instantaneous	1.45	2.53

Figure 115.—Type 94 (1934) 37-mm gun, with artillery wheels

Armor penetration, surface normal:

Projectile	Range (yards)	Penetration (inches)
Type 94 AP	0	2.1
Type 94 AP	250	1.9
Type 94 AP	500	1.7

Type 1 (1941) 47-mm Antitank Gun

This weapon, of modern design, is a very effective antitank gun, capable of a high rate of fire. It is issued for the most part to independent antitank and armored units, although it is gradually replacing the Type 94 (1934) 37-mm gun as the organic weapon of the regimental antitank gun company.

The barrel, of built-up construction, consists of a tube and jacket. The long tube has a heavy reinforced muzzle band, and employs a

Figure 116.—Type 1 (1941) 47-mm antitank gun.

semiautomatic, horizontal sliding breechblock. A hydrospring recoil mechanism is housed in a trough-type cradle which is trunnioned to the top carriage at about the point of balance. The long trail legs are of welded steel construction and open to an angle of 60 degrees for firing. The ends of the axle extend into a knee-action shock-absorbing assembly, held in a cylindrical housing. For firing, the shock-absorbing system is locked.

Figure 117.—Type 1 (1941) 47-mm antitank gun showing shape of shield.

Mounted on steel disc wheels fitted with sponge-rubber-filled tires, the weapon is highly mobile. It is well balanced, easy to manhandle, and can be rapidly brought in and out of action.

The sight used on the Type 1 (1941) 47-mm gun is a 7-power prismatic device with cross hairs graduated in 10-mil steps. On the right side of the gun, just behind the shield, is a range drum consisting of three dials. The dials on the right and left are graduated in hundreds of meters and represent the range to the target. The right dial is used with HE ammunition, the left with AP. The center dial is graduated in hundreds of meters and represents the range to the target. The right dial is used with HE ammunition, the left with AP. The

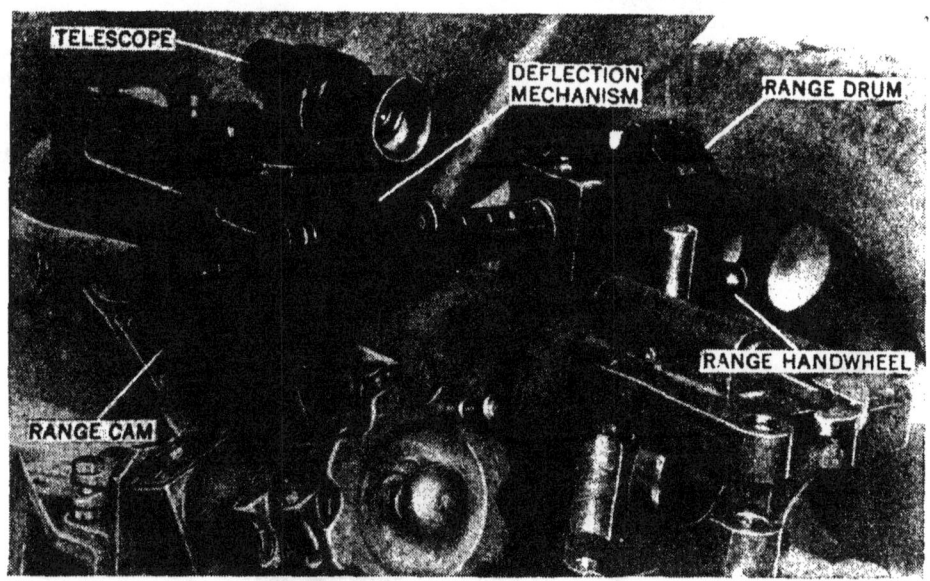

Figure 118.—Sighting mechanism of Type 1 (1941) 47-mm antitank gun.

center dial is graduated in 10-mil steps and gives angle of elevation. An open, mechanical sight may be substituted for the telescope.

The traversing and elevating mechanisms for the Type 1 are essentially the same as those on the Type 94. In direct firing, the gunner lays for both azimuth and elevation and fires the weapon by striking the plunger on the small elevating handwheel, which actuates the percussion hammer mechanism. On recoil, the firing mechanism is recocked, the breech is opened, and the spent shell case ejected.

SPECIFICATIONS:

Caliber	47 mm (1.85 inches).
Weight firing	1,660 pounds.
Length of tube	99.48 inches.
Traverse	60°.
Elevation	−11° to +19°.
Muzzle velocity	2,700 feet per second with AP.
Sight	Straight telescope.

Figure 119.—Type 1 (1941) 47-mm antitank gun, left side showing traversing and elevating handwheel and driven spades.

*Ammunition (fixed) or
Type 1 antitank gun:*

Projectile	Fuze	Weight (pounds)	Weight of Complete Round (pounds)
HE	Type 88 instantaneous	3.08	5.4
	Type 88 short delay	3.08	5.4
APHE	Mark II base short delay	3.37	6.1
Type 1: APHE			

Figure 120.—Type 97 (1937) 20-mm antitank rifle.

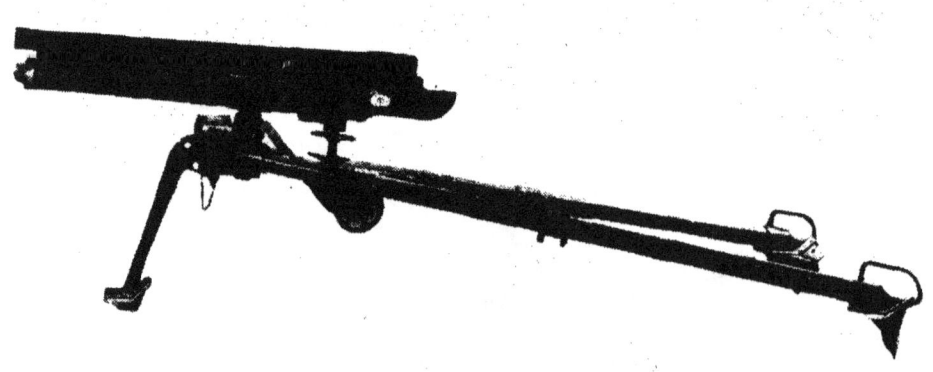

Figure 121.—Type 11 (1922) 37-mm gun.

Armor penetration of Type 1 antitank gun with APHE:

Range (yards)	Penetration in inches (Normal)	(30 degrees)
250	3.0	2.25
500	2.75	2.0
750	2.45	1.7
1,000	2.0	1.4
1,500	1.6	1.2

Figure 122.—Type 97 (1937) 37-mm gun.

Figure 123.—5-cm (47-mm) naval landing force gun.

Figure 124.—Type 92 (1932) 70-mm howitzer.

Figure 125.—Type 41 (1908) 75-mm gun.

Weapon	Muzzle Velocity (feet per second)	Weight of AP Projectile	Penetration	Traverse (degrees)	Elevation (degrees)	Type of Trail	Type of Spades	Remarks
Type 97 (1937), 20-mm Rifle.	2,600	5.72 ounces	1.18 inches at normal at 270 yards.	90	−5 to +5	(Traverse difficult.)		Found in infantry machine-gun company, armored-division rifle company; man-carried, may have shield.
Type 11 (1922), 37-mm Gun.	1,480	1.5 pounds		33	−5 to +14	Split	Integral	Replaced by Type 94. No shield, easily manhandled.
Type 94 (1934), 37-mm Gun.	2,327	1.54 pounds	1.9 inches at normal at 250 yards.	60	−10 to +27	Split	Driven	Substitute standard. May be packed by animal or manhandled.
Type 97 (1937), 37-mm Gun.	2,625	1.5 pounds		60	−8 to +25	Split	Integral	German Pak 37: apparently never adopted as standard.
Type 1 (1941), 47-mm Gun.	2,700	3.37 pounds	2.75 inches at normal at 500 yards.	63	−11 to +19	Split	Driven	Standard antitank gun: found in regimental antitank company, divisional antitank battalions.
5-cm (47-mm) Naval Landing Force Gun.				None	−11 to +2	Box	Driven or none.	Obsolete weapon.
Type 92 (1932), 70-mm Howitzer.	650	7.4 pounds (hollow charge).	3.1 inches	45	−11 to +70	Box	Integral	Found in battalion heavy weapons company; sighting by panoramic telescope.
Type 41 (1908), 75-mm Gun.	1,160	13.66 pounds (Type 95 AP HE), 7.81 pounds (Type 2 hollow charge).	2.75 inches with hollow charge.	6	−18 to +40	Box	Integral	Found in infantry regimental cannon company; sighting by panoramic telescope.

Figure 126.—Infantry and antitank guns in antitank roles.

Field Artillery

Adaptability of Field Artillery to Antitank Role

Handicapped by weapon designs largely unsuitable for an antitank role, the Japanese have nevertheless made consistent efforts to use field artillery against Allied armor. Their most pronounced success has been with the Type 90 (1930) 75-mm field gun, which in its mobile, pneumatic-tired version is a formidable antitank weapon. Its advantages over most other Japanese field pieces in an antitank role include a comparatively high muzzle velocity, and 50-degree traverse permitted by the pintle-type traversing mechanism and long, split trails. The driven spades, characteristic of all Japanese split-trail carriages, diminish this gun's antitank effectiveness, since trail shifting is a lengthy process.

The Type 90 and all the principal 75-mm field guns, as well as the Type 91 (1931) 105-mm howitzer, have elevating and traversing handwheels on the same side, facilitating direct laying on a moving target. But the Japanese have not as yet taken advantage of this design feature by equipping these guns with elbow telescopes or other suitable direct-laying sighting devices. The Japanese medium artillery weapons, which are in some cases supplied with AP ammunition, have the azimuth handwheel on the left side and the elevating handwheel on the right.

Ammunition

Three types of armor-piercing projectiles are furnished for the Japanese 75-mm field guns. These are the Type 95 (1935) APHE round weighing 13.66 pounds, the Type 1 (1941) APHE round weighing 14.6 pounds, and the Type 2 (1942) hollow-charge projectile, which weighs 8.2 pounds with fuze. It is believed that these three types of ammunition probably are furnished to all the principal 75-mm weapons. The Type 90 (1930) 75-mm gun uses a different cartridge case from that of the other Japanese 75-mm guns. The case used with the Type 90 is 16.5 inches long, while that used with the other 75-mm guns is 11.5 inches long.

It is known that the Type 94 (1934) 75-mm mountain gun fires all three armor-piercing projectiles with penetration, surface normal, as follows:

Armor penetration, surface normal:

Projectile	Range (yards)	Penetration (inches)
APHE (14.65 pounds)	300	2.8
APHE (14.65 pounds)	1,000	2.3
Hollow charge		3.5

Figure 127.—Type 92 (1932) 105-mm gun.

The Type 91 (1931) 105-mm howitzer, firing Type 1 APHE, at a muzzle velocity of 1,450 feet per second, at normal angle of impact, achieves the following penetrations:

Range (yards)	Penetration (inches)
250	2.95
500	2.8
750	2.7

Japanese medium artillery is not as likely to be met in an antitank role as the light field pieces. However, various medium guns are supplied with AP ammunition. The Type 92 (1932) 105-mm gun fires a Type 95 APHE projectile weighing 35 pounds. The Type 95 APHE projectile for the Type 4 (1915) 150-mm howitzer weighs 78.7 pounds. The Type 96 (1936) 150-mm howitzer, firing Type 1 APHE

Figure 128.—Type 96 (1936) 150-mm howitzer.

at a muzzle velocity of 1,640 feet per second, achieves the following penetrations at normal angle of impact:

Range (yards)	Penetration (inches)
250	4.9
500	4.7
750	4.4
1,000	4.0

Type 90 (1930) 75-mm Field Gun

This weapon, the most up-to-date of its kind produced by the Japanese, is used in both field and antitank roles. It has been produced in two types, one with wooden artillery wheels for horse draft, the other with small pneumatic-tired disc wheels for tractor or truck draft. The mobile version is capable of rapid movement and is issued

Figure 129.—Type 90 (1930) 75-mm gun, motorized version.

to armored units. It may be issued to independent field artillery units, while the horse-drawn type is issued to division artillery regiments.

The long monobloc tube has a horizontal sliding, hand-operated breechblock and is fitted with a muzzle brake. The muzzle brake has a single baffle plate with six ports for gas escape. The tube rides in a trough-type cradle, trunnioned 1 foot in front of the breech. Coil-spring equilibrators are fitted. Full elliptic springs, with nine leaves in each spring, are fitted to the carriage of the mobile version. For firing, two small, screw-type jacks, fitted between an upper and lower axle, are cranked down until the weight of the gun is supported on the lower axle through the jacks, and the springs are out of action. The gun is well balanced, and hence easy to manhandle.

The driven spades may be locked for action against moving targets to act as fixed spades.

Figure 130.—Type 90 (1930) 75-mm gun, horse-drawn version with driven spades in place.

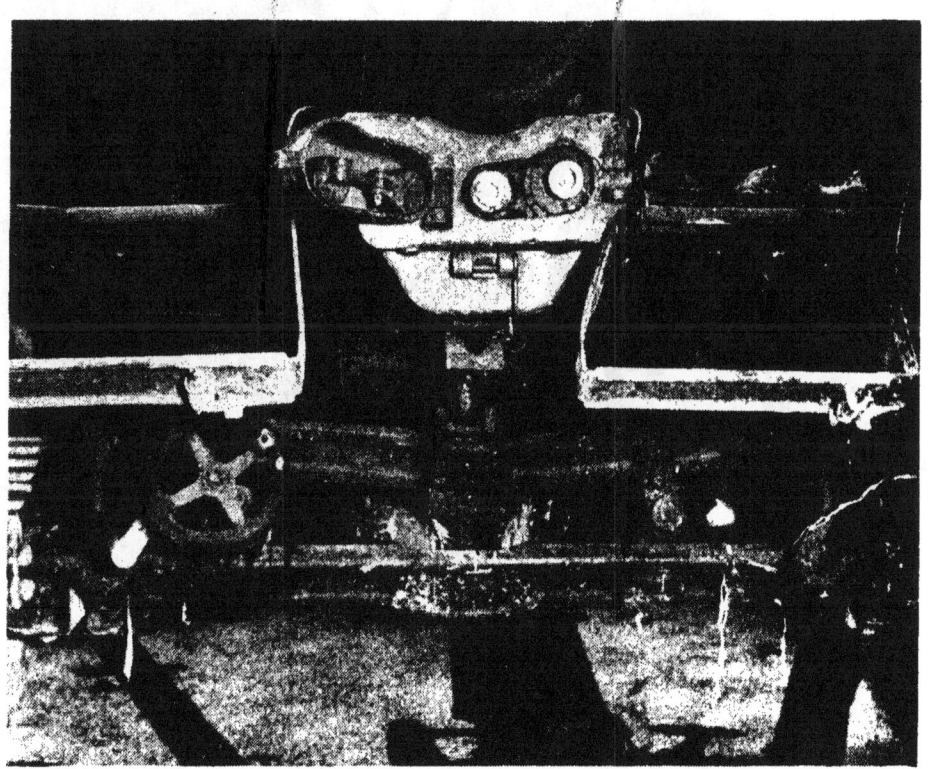

Figure 131.—Front view of lower carriage of Type 90 (1930) 75-mm gun, showing cranks for screw-type jacks. The crank on the left of the photo is partly concealed by the brake handwheel.

Figure 132.—Panoramic telescope, telescope mount, range drum, and elevating and traversing handwheels of the Type 90 (1930) 75-mm gun.

For sighting, the gun is equipped with the Type 95A panoramic telescope. It is also equipped with a range drum which has one scale in mils (0 to 750) and two scales graduated in meters The scale marked "I" is for long pointed HE shell and is marked from 0 to 14,000 meters (0 to 15,200 yards). The scale marked "II" is for the common HE shell, and is graduated from 0 to 9,200 meters (0 to 10,060 yards). The handwheels, located in close proximity to the panoramic telescope mount, are low geared. It is therefore difficult to make very rapid changes in azimuth and elevation.

SPECIFICATIONS:

Caliber	75 mm (2.95 inches).
Weight firing:	
Horse-drawn	3,080 pounds.
Tractor-drawn	3,520 pounds.
Length of tube	8 feet, 9 inches.
Traverse	50°.
Elevation	−8° to +45°.
Muzzle velocity	2,230 feet per second (pointed HE shell).
Rate of fire	10 to 12 rounds per minute.

AMMUNITION:

Projectile	Fuze	Weight (pounds)
Type 90 HE pointed	Type 88 instantaneous	14
Type 94 HE	Type 88 short delay	13.24
Type 95 APHE	Type 95 small bore	13.26
Type 1 APHE	Type 1 medium, short delay	14.6

Figure 133.—*Type 90 (1930) 75-mm gun as emplaced on Luzon. Note that the trails are not fully spread.*

Armor penetration with Type 1 APHE, surface normal:

Range (yards)	Penetration (inches)
250	3.5
500	3.3
750	3.0
1,000	2.8
1,500	2.4

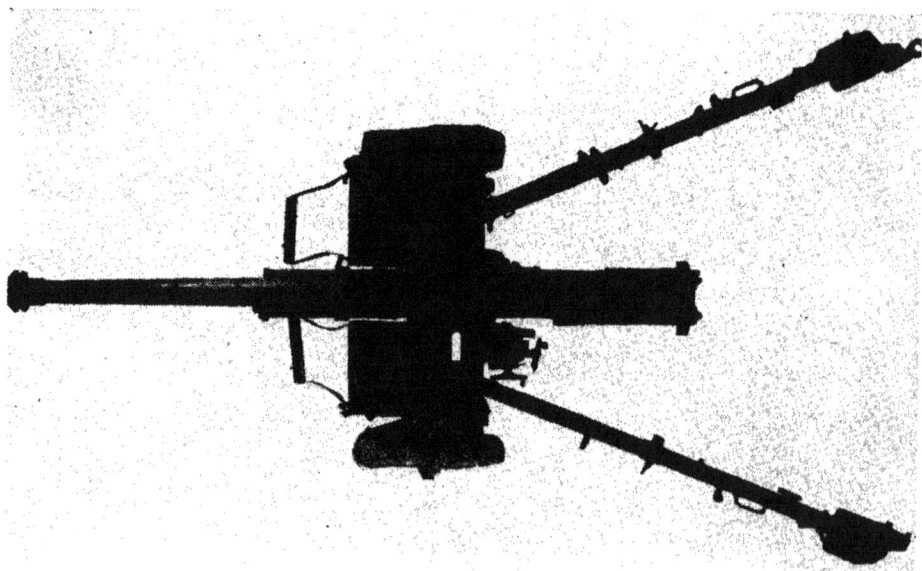

Figure 134.—Type 90 (1930) 75-mm gun, top view, with trails fully spread.

Figure 135.—Type 38 (1905) 75-mm gun in full recoil. Note muzzle blast.

Weapon	Muzzle Velocity (feet per second)	Traverse (degrees)	Elevation (degrees)	Type of Trail	Type of Spades	Remarks
Type 38 (1905), 75-mm gun.	------	7	−8 to +16½	Box	Integral	Replaced as divisional artillery weapon by improved version; now used in fixed emplacements.
Type 38 (1905), 75-mm gun Improved.	1,670	7	−8 to +43	Modified Box	Integral	Division artillery weapon.
Type 41 (1908), 75-mm cavalry gun.	1,673	12	−8 to +16½	Box	Integral	Similar to original Type 38.
Type 90 (1930), 75-mm gun.	2,230	50	−8 to +45	Split	Driven	Tractor-drawn; armored units and independent field artillery regiments; horse-drawn; division artillery units.
Type 94 (1934), 75-mm mountain gun.	1,475	40	−8 to +45	Split	Driven	Mountain artillery units.
Type 95 (1935), 75-mm gun.	1,700	50	−8 to +43	Split	Driven	Designed to replace Type 38 Improved.
Type 91 (1931), 105-mm howitzer.	1,450	40	−5 to +45	Split	Driven	Division artillery units.

Figure 136.—Light field artillery guns in antitank roles.

Figure 137.—Type 38 (1905) 75-mm gun, rear view showing solid box trail.

Figure 138.—Type 38 (1905) improved 75-mm gun.

Figure 139.—Type 38 (1905) improved 75-mm gun, top view showing open box trail.

Figure 140.—Type 41 (1908) 75-mm cavalry gun with box trail and interrupted-screw breechblock.

Figure 141.—Type 94 (1934) 75-mm mountain gun.

Figure 142.—Type 95 (1935) 75-mm gun.

Figure 143.—Type 95 (1935) 75-mm gun, top view with trails spread.

Figure 144.—Type 91 (1931) 105-mm howitzer.

Antiaircraft Artillery

Estimate in Antitank Role

Like Japanese field artillery, their heavy antiaircraft guns frequently have been found emplaced to cover beaches and likely tank approaches with direct fire and have occasionally been used against Allied tanks with good effect. Armor-piercing projectiles are now being issued for use with the Type 88 (1938) 75-mm and Type 99 (1939) 88-mm antiaircraft guns, and it is probable that a similar issue is being made for the Type 10 (1921) 120-mm dual-purpose naval gun. In addition, tanks may be put out of action if hit in a vulnerable spot by the usual antiaircraft HE ammunition.

For antitank purposes, the antiaircraft guns have the advantages of high muzzle velocity and all-around traverse, but the disadvantage of limited mobility. The Type 10 120-mm gun has the additional advantage of speed-ring sights, which assist in tracking moving ground targets. The Type 99 (1939) 88-mm gun is equipped with open sights for ground fire, while the Type 88 (1928) 75-mm gun has elbow telescopes. The Japanese antiaircraft guns can be effective when fired from ambush against tanks, but they cannot shoot and run. The Type 11 and Type 88 75-mm guns and the Type 14 105-mm weapon are on mobile mounts; which, however, do not allow the rapid shift of firing position desirable in antitank warfare. The other known Japanese heavy antiaircraft guns, including naval types, are on fixed mounts.

The Type 11 (1922) 75-mm gun is now obsolete as an antiaircraft weapon, but it still may be encountered, with a shield, in fixed defenses. It fires the same projectile as the 75-mm field guns, indicating that it is probably supplied with armor-piercing and perhaps hollow-charge ammunition.

The Navy's heavy antiaircraft guns may be effective as antitank weapons, despite their lack of mobility. Recent information indicates that gun sections manning the fixed-mount, naval, dual-purpose guns, used principally for antiaircraft fire, and the Type 4 150-mm howitzer are to be furnished with improvised mortars and sets of special fuzes so that, even though the gun may be knocked out or rendered unserviceable, the ammunition may still be fired. It is possible that all types of Japanese artillery sections will be equipped with these emergency mortars, which could damage tank tracks by firing artillery ammunition.

Use of Automatic Weapons in Antitank Role

Automatic weapons, intended primarily for antiaircraft fire but which are used against tanks and other ground targets, include the Type 93 (1933) 13.2-mm machine gun, used by both the Japanese Army and Navy, the Army Type 98 (1938) 20-mm machine cannon, and the Navy Type 96 (1936) 25-mm machine cannon. Armor-piercing ammunition is issued for all three weapons. The 25-mm gun, in single, twin, and triple mounts, is the most effective against armor. The normal Navy mount for this weapon is a fixed pedestal, but the Japanese have attempted to give it needed mobility on land by placing it on improvised sled or trailer mobile mounts. The computing or speed-ring sights on these automatic weapons are suitable for tracking moving ground targets. The Vickers 40-mm gun is largely ineffective against tanks because of its low muzzle velocity.

Type 98 (1938) 20-mm Machine Cannon

This is the standard mobile antiaircraft automatic weapon used by the Japanese Army antiaircraft units. The weapon is used in an antitank role as well as for antiaircraft defense. On a two-wheel mount, it can be towed by a vehicle, manhandled, or broken down

Figure 145.— Type 98 (1938) 20-mm machine cannon.

and carried in pack. Normally fired from its three outriggers, it also can be fired from its wheels, but performance under these conditions naturally is impaired.

The gunner elevates the weapon by a handwheel at the left rear and traverses by pressing on the shoulder rest.

SPECIFICATIONS:

Caliber	20 mm (0.787 inch).
Length of tube	57.5 inches (with muzzle brake).
Weight firing	835 pounds (without wheels).
Traverse	360° (without wheels).
Elevation	$-10°$ to $+85°$.
Muzzle velocity	3,000 feet per second.

AMMUNITION:

Projectile	Weight (ounces)	Weight of Complete Rouud (ounces)
HE tracer	4.8	14.3
AP tracer	5.72	15.2

Type 96 (1936) 25-mm Machine Cannon (Navy)

This naval weapon is a combined recoil- and blowback-operated, magazine-fed, automatic and semiautomatic machine cannon. It is found in single, twin, and triple mounts. The twin and triple versions have heavily constructed, deck-type pedestal mounts. In land emplacements, this mount is fastened to a heavy iron base which is buried in the ground. The single-barrel versions are usually found on simple, fixed, pedestal mounts. Improvised mobile mounts also

Figure 146.—Type 96 (1936) 25-mm machine cannon, single-mount, mobile version.

Figure 147.—Type 96 (1936) 25-mm machine cannon, single-mount, pedestal-mounted version on improvised sled.

have been found. Single and twin mounts have been placed on sleds, while the twin mount has been placed on four-wheel trailers. The single-barrel gun has also been found on a wheeled mount.

These automatic cannons are widely used, and have been found emplaced in defense of airstrips adjacent to port and harbor installations, manned by naval shore-based personnel. They are usually emplaced for defense against both air and ground attacks, as the weapon can be used very effectively against all types of ground targets. The twin-mount version is commonly equipped with a speed-ring sight which can be used for direct fire against ground targets. It is laid by means of two handwheels, one on each side of the gun. The

Figure 148.—Type 96 (1936) 25-mm machine cannon, single-mount, emplaced in artificial cave on Luzon.

single 25-mm is mounted free and moved by the gunner at will. It uses a speed-ring sight exclusively.

SPECIFICATIONS:

Caliber	25 mm (0.98 inches).
Weight firing	5,330 pounds (three guns).
Traverse	360°.
Elevation	$-10°$ to $+85°$
Muzzle velocity	2,850 feet per second.
Practical rate of fire	190 rounds per minute (per barrel).

AMMUNITION:

Projectile	Weight (ounces)	Weight of Complete Round (ounces)
HE	8.20	24.12
HE tracer	8.56	23.23
AP tracer	10	25.2

The Type 96 (1936) 25-mm machine cannon is known to have an armor penetration of at least 2.36 inches at 500 yards.

Figure 149.—Type 96 (1936) 25-mm machine cannon, twin-mount version on improvised sled.

Figure 150.—Type 96 (1936) 25-mm machine cannon, twin mount version on improvised sled, rear view.

Type 88 (1928) 75-mm Antiaircraft Gun

Designated by the Japanese as the 7-cm field antiaircraft gun, this weapon represents the standard mobile antiaircraft gun with which the Japanese entered the war. It is fitted with elbow telescopes, which facilitate tracking of moving targets.

The tube is of the built-up type, with one reinforcing jacket which contains the breech ring and extends for two-thirds of the length of the barrel. The breech mechanism is of the horizontal-sliding-wedge type. Recoil is hydropneumatic, variable.

Figure 151.—Type 88 (1928) 75-mm antiaircraft gun, zero elevation.

Mounted on a pedestal with five folding outriggers, the weapon is transported on two rubber-tired wheels. It can be put into action from traveling position with rapidity, but frequent changes of firing position are not normally made. It closely resembles its predecessor, the Type 11 (1922) 75-mm gun.

SPECIFICATIONS:

Caliber	75 mm (2.95 inches).
Length of tube	10 feet, 10 inches.
Weight firing	5,400 pounds.
Traverse	360°.
Elevation	$-7°$ to $+85°$.
Muzzle velocity	2,360 feet per second.
Rate of fire	10 to 15 rounds per minute.

AMMUNITION (FIXED):

Projectile	Fuze	Weight (pounds)	Weight of Complete Round (pounds)
Type 90 HE AA pointed	Type 89 AA	14.37	19.7
Type 90 HE pointed	Type 88 instantaneous, Type 88 short delay.	14.0	18.85
Type 95 APHE	Type 95 small base	13.66	----

Figure 152.—Type 88 (1928) 75-mm antiaircraft gun, maximum elevation.

Figure 153.—Type 88 (1928) 75-mm antiaircraft gun, partial traveling position.

Armor penetration with AP projectile:

Range (yards)	Penetration (inches)
100	3.75
500	3.6
1,000	3.15
1,500	2.75

Figure 154.—*Type 88 (1928) 75-mm antiaircraft gun in action against ground targets in China (1938). Note mortar at left of gun position.*

Type 10 (1921) 120-mm Dual-Purpose Gun (Navy)

This Navy dual-purpose gun has been found on the important islands of the Pacific where it was occasionally used against tanks with good effect. Originally designed for shipborne use, the weapon was manufactured in large numbers by the Japanese Navy in 1944.

The gun has a relatively high muzzle velocity and utilizes a semi-automatic, horizontal sliding-wedge breechblock. Two hydropneumatic recoil cylinders are mounted above the tube with a small buffer cylinder between them. The gun is mounted on a conical steel pedestal of standard naval design, which necessitates either a wooden or steel spider. The spiders are covered with earth or concrete.

Efficient speed-ring sights are standard for this gun, and are retained even though data receivers are fitted for director control.

SPECIFICATIONS:
```
Caliber_____ 120 mm (4.72 inches).
Length of tube_____ 17 feet, 7.5 inches.
Total weight (approx.)_____ 8.5 tons.
Traverse_____ 360°.
Elevation_____ −5° to +75°.
Muzzle velocity_____ 2,700 feet per second.
Practical rate of fire_____ 10 rounds per minute.
```

The Type 10 Navy gun fires fixed HE and incendiary-shrapnel projectiles weighing 45.5 pounds. A complete round weighs 71.5 pounds. It is likely that AP ammunition is also available for this gun.

Figure 155.—Type 10 (1921) 120-mm dual-purpose gun (Navy). Note speed-ring sight. The emplacement wall is marked every 45 degrees to speed initial laying.

Figure 156.—Type 10 (1921) 120-mm dual-purpose gun (Navy). The emplacement wall is marked for every 5 degrees.

Figure 157.— Type 93 (1933) 13.2-mm machine gun on tripod.

Weapon	Muzzle Velocity (feet per second)	Weight of AP Projectile	Effective Rate of Fire (rounds per minute)	Sights	Mount
Type 93 (1933), 13.2-mm Machine Gun.	2,280	1.76 ounces	250 to 300 (per barrel).	Blade and leaf, or ring and bead for single barrel, slant-plane-linkage for twin barrel.	Pedestal or tripod; one or two barrels.
Type 98 (1938), 20-mm Machine Cannon.	3,000	5.72 ounces	120	Slant-lane-linkage computing.	Mobile, one-barrel.
Type 96 (1936), 25-mm Navy Gun.	2,850	10 ounces	190 (per barrel)	Slant-plane-linkage computing and speed-ring.	Fixed pedestal or improvised mobile sled or trailer; one, two, or three barrels.
Vickers, 40-mm Gun	1,968	2 pounds (approx.)	60 (per barrel)	Course and speed computing.	Fixed; one or two barrels.

Figure 158.—Antiaircraft automatic weapons in antitank roles.

Figure 159.— Type 93 (1933) 13.2-mm machine gun on twin-mount tripod.

Figure 160.— Vickers 40-mm gun, single-mount.

Figure 161.— Vickers 40-mm gun, twin-mount.

Weapon	Muzzle Velocity (feet per second)	Effective Rate of Fire (rounds per minute)	Mount
Type 11 (1922), 75-mm Army Gun.	1,750	10 to 12	Mobile or fixed pedestal.
Type 88 (1928), 75-mm Army Gun.	2,360	10 to 15	Mobile.
Type 3 (1914), 76.2-mm Navy Gun.	2,200	12	Fixed pedestal.
Type 99 (1939), 88-mm Army Gun.	[1] 2,625	——	Fixed.
Type 98 (1938), 100-mm Navy Gun.	3,280	——	Fixed, two barrels, splinter shield.
Type 14 (1905), 105-mm Army Gun.	2,300	10	Mobile.
Type 10 (1921), 120-mm Navy Gun.	2,700	10	Fixed, splinter shield.
Type 89 (1929), 127-mm Navy Gun.	2,360	12 (per barrel)	Fixed, two barrels, splinter shield.

[1] Estimated.

Figure 162.— Heavy antiaircraft guns in antitank roles.

Figure 163.— Type 11 (1922) 75-mm Army gun.

Figure 164.— Type 3 (1914) 76.2-mm Navy gun.

Figure 165.— Type 99 (1939) 88-mm Army gun.

Figure 166.— Type 98 (1938) 100-mm Navy gun.

Figure 167.— Type 14 (1905) 105-mm Army gun.

Figure 168.— Type 89 (1929) 127-mm Navy gun.

Coast Defense Artillery

The most common Japanese coast defense guns are naval weapons on pedestal-type, fixed mounts. They are capable of 360-degree traverse, although this is frequently restricted by the type emplacement, since they are now frequently found in caves.

Three general types of on-carriage fire control equipment will be found on the Japanese coast defense guns which are most likely to be used against Allied armor at landing beaches. The 76.2-mm and 120-mm Armstrong-type guns are laid directly with a telescope, combined with range scales. The gunner sits on the left side of the gun to operate both the elevating and traversing handwheels. The gunner for the 150-mm, 40-caliber, Armstrong-type weapon also sits on the left side and uses an elevation handwheel while he traverses the gun with a bicycle-type pedal arrangement. This gun has both open sights and a telescope. The other weapons considered here (Type 3 (1914) 120-mm gun, Type 11 (1922) 120-mm gun, Type 3 (1914) 140-mm gun, Type 41 (1908) 150-mm, 45- and 50-caliber guns) require two men for laying in direct fire, one man at the elevation handwheel on the left and the other at the traversing handwheel on the right, with voice-tube intercommunication. These weapons have both open sights and telescopes.

AP ammunition is probably issued for most, if not all, of these coast defense guns, which are all naval pieces. However, detailed information is not available on AP projectiles.

Weapon	Muzzle velocity (feet per second)	Weight of HE projectile (pounds)	Elevation (degrees)	Shield
76.2-mm Gun, Armstrong Type.	2,260	13.8 (HE)	−5 to +20	None.
120-mm Gun, Armstrong Type.	2,160	45	20	No shield recovered.
Type 3 (1914), 120-mm Gun.	2,700	45	−5 to +34	Light splinter shield only.
Type 11 (1922), 120-mm. Gun.	2,700	45	−10 to +50	Light splinter shield only.
Type 3 (1914), 140-mm Gun.	2,790	83.6 to 85.6	−7 to +30	Light cruiser-type or heavier battleship type.
150-mm 40-caliber Gun.	2,300	95	23	Cruiser-types proof against .50 caliber AP ammunition.
Type 41 (1908), 150-mm 45-caliber Gun.	2,700	95	−5 to +30	No shields recovered.
Type 41 (1908), 150-mm 50-caliber Gun.	2,790	95 (approx.)	−5 to +15	No shields recovered.

Figure 169.—Coast artillery in antitank roles.

Figure 170.—Type 3 (1914) 120-mm gun.

Figure 171.—Type 3 (1914) 140-mm gun with light cruiser-type shield.

Figure 172.—Type 3 (1914) 140-mm gun, with heavy battleship casemate-type shield.

Figure 173.—150-mm, 40-caliber gun with cruiser-type shield proof against caliber .50 AP ammunition.

Chapter IV. Antitank Mines, Rifle Grenades, and Flame Throwers

Antitank Mines

Introduction

In contrast to their former allies, the Japanese, prior to 1941, failed to appreciate fully the possibilities of mines, demolition charges, and flame throwers as means of bolstering antitank defenses. By and large, their originally inadequate appreciation of the menace of armored warfare was as marked in this field of engineer matériel as it was in weapons and tactics. The mines which were standard in the Japanese Army at the beginning of the war proved too light to be effective by Allied standards. The value of antilifting devices, and the proper use of booby traps and antipersonnel mines to protect antitank minefields, were little understood. Likewise, the capabilities of the various magnetic and other hollow-charge devices used by the Germans against Soviet armor were largely unrealized by the Japanese while they still had time to take remedial action on a comprehensive scope.

When the demonstrated potency of Allied armor compelled the Japanese to seek more effective countermeasures, the strain on their industrial potential was already so great as to preclude satisfaction of field requirements on a scale comparable with the Germans. The result has been the appearance of a great number of improvisations of both standardized and field expedient types.

Improvisations have been invoked to increase the power of antitank mines, as well as to increase the number of such devices. Typical of the standard types of officially-manufactured improvisations are the Type 3 (1943) mines, one model of which is made of pottery and the other of wood in order to make detection more difficult and perhaps also in order to conserve metals. Field improvisations often have sought to provide very powerful antitank mines by converting

Navy depth charges, artillery projectiles, and aerial bombs to antitank use. The Japanese are continuing to display typical ingenuity, persistence, and bravery in this type of antitank warfare. Nonetheless they are handicapped by inferior material, although the crudeness of the various types of hollow charges and demolition charges is offset, to a degree, by the cunning and suicidal fanaticism with which the Japanese soldier handles them.

Type 93 (1933) Mine

The Type 93 (1933) mine, usually known as the tape-measure mine because it resembles a rolled-up steel tape measure, consists of a tan or olive-drab circular metal casing in two halves. Two brass strips are soldered to diametrically opposite sides of the upper half, each carrying two brass "D" rings used for anchoring or carrying the mine. To the center of the bottom is soldered an internally-threaded brass disc, 0.56 inch in diameter, to which the detonator assembly is screwed. A central hole in the upper portion is reinforced with a brass collar, threaded to receive a milled brass plug. The overlap of the two halves of the cover is sealed.

The explosive filling is in two parts. A primer consisting of an annular pellet of pressed picric acid surrounds the detonator cavity. The main filling consists of a cylindrical slab of cast picric acid with a central perforation for the igniter assembly.

SPECIFICATIONS:

Diameter of mine	6.75 inches.
Height of mine	1.75 inches (approx.).
Weight of mine	3 pounds (approx.).
Weight of filling	2 pounds (approx.).

Figure 174.— Type 93 (1933) mine (tape-measure mine).

Type 93 (1933) Mine Fuze

The fuze assembly consists of a brass cylinder, provided with a centrally perforated transverse piece to act as a striker-guide. A steel plug screws into the top of this cylinder, and is drilled internally to take the steel striker and spring. A shear wire passes through a 0.093-inch diameter hole in the striker and steel plug, and is capable of taking a dead load of about 250 pounds; a more sensitive antipersonnel shear wire, which shears under a pressure of 25 to 70 pounds, is sometimes substituted. The upper end of the striker is drilled and threaded to take a brass safety cap, which when screwed home takes the pressure of the spring-loaded striker off the shear wire. A brass cylinder fits over this safety cap forming an additional safety device; it has a lug indicator with the Japanese ideograph for "safe" on it.

Pressure on the striker bolt shears the shear wire, which causes the striker to set down on the detonator and fires the mine. In order to neutralize the mine, antihandling devices first must be neutralized. The brass plug then is unscrewed without moving the mine or exerting any pressure on it. If the brass safety cap is available, it should be screwed firmly into the top of the striker. If neither is available, the fuze should be removed.

Yardstick Mine

The body of the yardstick mine is formed by two bent sheet-steel rectangles, seam-welded along their length to form an oval tube. Both ends of this tube are covered by removable steel caps, one of which is provided with a threaded hole for the safety wire and a spring clip to hold the latter in place. The caps are fixed to the tube by single screws.

The explosive charge is made up of eight equal, specially shaped blocks of picric acid. The blocks are cylinders conforming to the oval cross section of the body, but flattened on one side to allow space for the pressure plate of the fuze inside the tube. Each block has a shaped semicircular recess, approximately 1 inch in diameter, which allows two of the blocks, placed with these recesses adjoining, to retain one fuze between them. Four such pairs form the mine charge.

SPECIFICATIONS:

Mine body length	91 cm (36 inches).
Cross section (elliptical)	8.5 by 4.5 cm (3.35 by 1.8 inches).
Weight of body	2.1 kilograms (4.5 pounds).
Weight of charge	2.7 kilograms (6 pounds).
Total weight of mine	4.8 kilograms (10.5 pounds).
Size of charge blocks	11 by 8 by 3 cm (4.3 by 3.1 by 1.2 inches).
Firing pressure (provisional)	336 pounds.

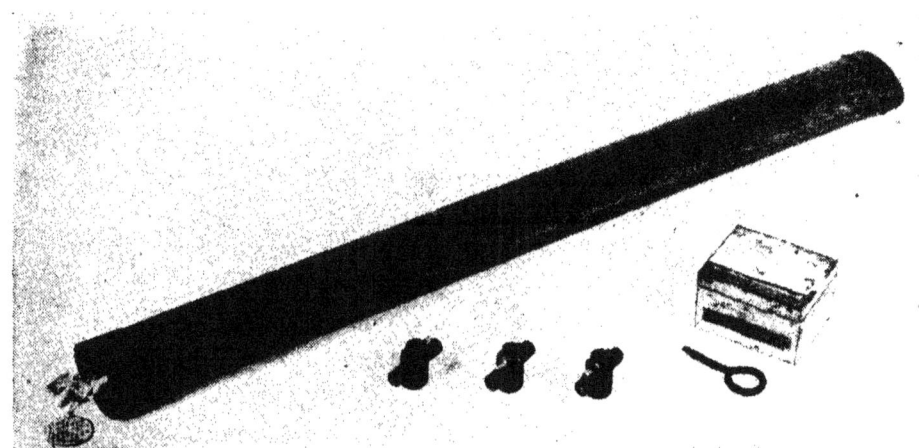

Figure 175.— Yardstick mine.

Yardstick Mine Fuze

The fuze is made of black-finished, rust-resistant steel, except for the copper shear wire. It is a single, compact, mechanical-action fuze, cross-shaped when completely assembled with striker and primer. The fuze body consists of a short cylinder which houses the release plunger, and has two threaded holes on opposite sides. Into one side is screwed the striker assembly, consisting of striker housing, striker, and striker spring; into the other side is screwed the primer assembly, consisting of the primer in its holder, and the percussion cap. The striker housing and primer holder are steel cylinders of the same size and outside finish, but the primer holder is marked with a daub of red paint on the base to distinguish it. Instead of a detonator, there is an initiator charge pressed directly into the yellowish-white primer.

The striker release plunger is shaped as a split pin, 1.5 inches long and about 0.3 inch thick, with an enlarged flat head about 1 inch in diameter. It has a perforation to take the safety wire, and a little below this there is another hole, at 90 degrees to the first, to accommodate the copper shear wire. The slot, which is cut lengthwise out of the lower half of the plunger, is about 0.078 inch wide at the bottom, sufficient to take the firing pin. The slot opens out to about 0.172 inch at its inner end, sufficient to take the striker shaft.

The striker itself is a one-piece steel piston turned down to three different diameters to form the head, shaft, and firing pin. The striker spring is a short compression coil spring of the same diameter as the striker head.

When sufficient force is applied to the mine body to depress the fuze pressure head, it will sever the copper shear wire and depress the striker release plunger. The enlarged portion of the slot in the plunger is moved down and allows the striker shaft to drive through the opening. The striker pin hits the percussion cap and thus detonates the initiator, primer charge, and so the main charge.

Any antihandling devices first must be neutralized in neutralizing the mine. The end cap then is removed, after which the charge is carefully slid out until the fuze becomes visible. A nail then is inserted across the safety wire hole. This procedure must be repeated for all fuzes in the mine.

Type 98 (1938) Hemispherical Antiboat Mine

This mine, designed by the Japanese for beach defense against landing craft, is also used on land as an antitank mine. It is of a hemispherical appearance, with two protruding, horn-like, electrochemical igniters.

The mild steel body has welded to it two carrying handles, and two internally-trapped sockets for the two fuzes; centrally, on top, is the plunger-contact-assembly socket. The base plate, welded 0.81 inch above the rim, has a filling hole closed by a right-hand threaded

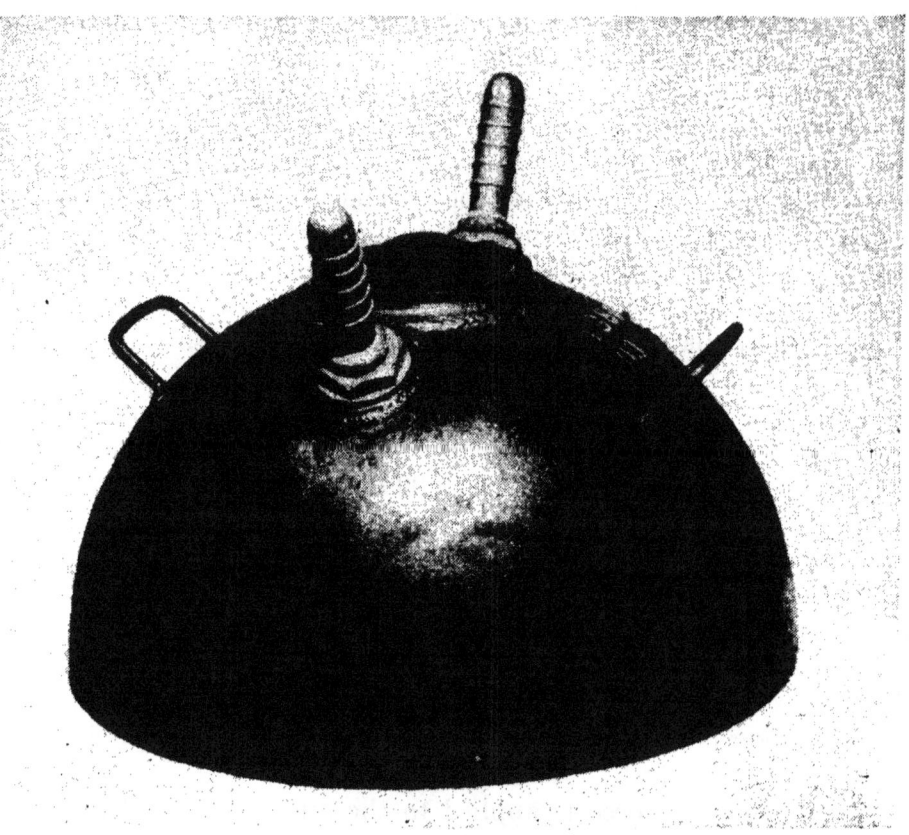

Figure 176.— Type 98 (1938) hemispherical antiboat mine.

plug. A horizontal plate divides the inside of the body into two compartments. The top compartment contains the plunger contact assembly, the two fuzes, and the connecting wiring. The lower compartment contains the main explosive charge.

SPECIFICATIONS:

Diameter at base	20.50 inches.
Height	10.62 inches.
Thickness of body	0.18 inch.
Weight of mine (less fuzes)	106.50 pounds.
Weight of explosive	46.50 pounds.
Type of explosive (main charge booster)	Trinitroanisol (T.N.A.), picric acid.
Dimensions of fuze sockets:	
Diameter across threads	1.69 inches.
Depth to inner shoulder	1.13 inches.
Diameter across inner shoulder	1.50 inches.
Dimensions of plunger-assembly socket:	
Diameter across threads	5.06 inches.
Depth to inner shoulder	1.12 inches.
Diameter across inner shoulder	4.12 inches.

Plunger Contact Assembly

This consists of a cylindrical body screwed to the underside of the cover plate which is screwed into the socket, and locked by a ring. The spring-loaded striker is assembled with the cover plate. In the unarmed position, the plunger is held upwards through the cover plate, against a spring, by a safety fork. The plunger can be retracted from the armed to the unarmed position by means of a retracting pin.

When the safety fork is withdrawn, the plunger, under the influence of its spring, comes into contact with the blade on the terminals. In the base of the assembly is an electric detonator fitted into a picric acid booster.

The detonator is wired in series with the terminals and igniters so that the activation of either cell will close the circuit.

To arm the mine, the plunger contact assembly is removed; the picric booster, detonator, and wiring are coupled to the terminals; and the assembly is replaced. The fuzes (horns) then are inserted with the plunger in the unarmed position. After the mine is laid the safety fork is removed.

To neutralize the mine, the retracting pin is screwed into the head of the plunger and pulled upwards. The safety fork then is inserted in the grooves on the plunger.

Type 98 (1938) Antiboat Mine Fuze

The fuze used with the Type 98 antiboat mine consists of a horn of lead alloy casting, the base of which has a turned thread for screwing into the socket. The external surface of the horn is corrugated at approximately half-inch intervals. A glass vial, held in position by a coiled spring, contains a chemical solution. Held in the lower shoulders of the socket is an electric cell consisting of a zinc cathode (negative) and a carbon anode (positive). This cell is capable of a maximum current of 4 amperes at 1.8 volts and has an internal resistance of 0.397 ohm.

When the lead alloy horn is distorted or crushed, the glass vial inside is broken, and the solution passes into the cell and thereby sets up an electromotive force. The current thus produced passes to the detonator, causing the mine to explode.

Single-Horn Antiboat Mine (Tea-kettle Mine)

This mine, besides having only one horn, differs from the Type 98 antiboat mine in shape. The steel case, in the shape of a truncated cone, has welded to it two carrying handles and a base plate. The latter has a filling hole with a screw-on cover in the center. A horizontal plate, welded to the inside of the case, divides it into two compartments. The top compartment contains the firing mechanism, the lower the main explosive charge.

The top aperture of the mine is closed by a mechanism plate, which holds the firing mechanism and is retained by a keep ring.

SPECIFICATIONS:

Diameter at base	14.25 inches.
Diameter at top	7.00 inches.
Height (to top of horn)	16.14 inches.
Weight of mine (fully equipped)	65 to 70 pounds.
Weight of explosive	22 pounds.
Type of explosive:	
Main charge	Trinitroanisol, 60 percent.
	Dipicrylamine, 40 percent.
Primer	Picric acid.

Plunger Contact Assembly

The plunger contact assembly is similar to that of the Type 98 hemispherical antiboat mine, but set together in the mechanism plate. The mine is armed by the same procedure as used for the Type 98 mine. Neutralization is accomplished by unscrewing the keep ring and removing the mechanism plate and firing mechanism. After all electric leads are disconnected, the primer, detonator, and electric cell are removed, and the mechanism plate is replaced.

Figure 177.—Single-horn antiboat mine (tea-kettle mine).

Type 3 (1943), Model A, Land Mine (Pottery Mine)

This mine, manufactured in two sizes, has a terra cotta case, the exterior of which has a dull glazed finish, while the inner surface is highly glazed. Within the case is a light rubber bag containing the explosive filler. Inserted and sealed in the center of the mine-case top is a threaded rubber fuze seating.

SPECIFICATIONS:

	Large Model	*Small Model*
Diameter	10.5 inches	8.5 inches.
Height	3.5 inches	3.5 inches.
Weight of filling	6.5 pounds (approx.).	4.5 pounds (approx.).
Types of filling	(1) Amatol 50/50 percent.	
	(2) Ammonium nitrate 90 percent, and dinitronaphthalene 10 percent.	
	(3) Ammonium perchlorate, ferro silicon, sawdust, and crude oil, 75, 16, 6, and 3 percent respectively.	

Figure 178.— Type 3 (1943), Model A land mine (pottery mine).

Type 3 (1943) Land Mine Fuze

The Type 3 fuze is a combination pull-and-pressure fuze. It consists of a bakelite body of two parts. The lower part, threaded to fit the fuze pocket of the mine, holds a metal striker, percussion cap, and detonator tube. The upper part houses a bakelite plunger body fitting over a spring. This plunger body, in turn, holds a percussion hammer, held in position against the pressure of a small spring by a light metal release fork. A safety pin, passing through the bakelite head, prevents downward movement of the plunger body in the unarmed position.

Another Type 3 land mine fuze, slightly different in design, has been recovered. It has two annular grooves in a bakelite body and threads into the fuze seating with left-hand threads. The top of the pressure plate has a straight-line design, and the safety pin passes through a hole in the percussion hammer.

When armed by removal of the safety pin, pressure of about 26 to 40 pounds compresses the main plunger spring, and the plunger group moves downwards into the head of the striker, thus firing the mine.

As a secondary method of firing, a trip wire fixed to the release fork is employed. A direct pull of 4 to 5 pounds causes the removal of the fork. The small spring of the percussion hammer then forces the latter downward into the head of the striker, thus firing the mine.

Neutralization is effected by inserting a safety pin or small nail in the safety-pin hole. If a trip wire is attached, it should be cut before unscrewing the fuze from the mine body.

Type 3 (1943), Model B, Land Mine (Box Mine)

This other version of the Type 3 consists of a factory-made wooden box, sides of which are box-jointed and nailed, and the lid of which is fastened with 1-inch screws. A rubber fuze socket is attached to a hole in the top into which is set the combination pull-pressure Model 3 land mine fuze. The explosive charge is contained inside the box in a light rubber bag.

Figure 179.— Type 3 (1943), Model B, land mine (box mine).

SPECIFICATIONS:

Length	7.125 inches.
Width	7.125 inches.
Height	4.875 inches.
Weight	6.250 pounds.
Weight of explosive	4.50 pounds.
Type of explosive	Type 88.
	Ammonium perclorate, 66 percent.
	Silicon carbide, 16 percent.
	Wood pulp, 12 percent.
	Oil, 6 percent.

Type 4 (1944) Land Mine

This mine is known to exist, from documentary evidence, but few details are known. It is said that when buried in the ground this mine can be used as a time or remote control mine. It cannot be detected by a mine detector because the charge is contained in a wooden box, and the fuze is made of bakelite.

SPECIFICATIONS:

Igniter	Instantaneous and delay pressure.
Weight of charge	64 pounds.
Size	12.6 by 12.6 by 12.6 inches.
Weight fully equipped	83 pounds.

Shoulder-Pack Antitank Mine

This mine is a wooden box, about 11 inches square, weighing between 15 and 20 pounds. It is equipped with rope shoulder straps. The mine has a pull cord of copper wire, about 36 inches long, with a wooden grip attached. This cord is attached to the safety pin of the fuze in the top of the mine.

A soldier straps the mine on his back and conceals himself near the path of an approaching tank. When the tank arrives at a suitable distance, the soldier dashes forward, throws himself between the tracks, and pulls the cord. The mine explodes in 1 to 3 seconds.

Lunge Antitank Mine

The conical case of the lunge mine is made of unpainted steel. Three legs attached to the base give a stand-off of 6 inches. At the apex is either a standard grenade-detonator or a primer cap, safety fuze, and detonator. Screwed to the apex is a metal tube containing a long wooden pole with a pointed striker at the lower end. The pole and striker are held away from the detonator by a safety pin and a copper shear wire. The liner of the cone is made of aluminum or steel.

SPECIFICATIONS:

Weight of mine body	11.8 pounds.
Weight of charge	6.40 pounds.
Length of mine body	11 inches.
Diameter at base	8 inches.
Length of handle	76 inches.
Internal height of shaped-charge cone	4.5 inches.
Bottom diameter of cone	3.7 inches.
Apex angle	40°.

After removing the safety pin, the attacker lunges forward toward the target, with sufficient force to shear the shear wire and drive the striker into the cap. It is reported that this mine is capable of penetrating 6 inches of armor plate with head-on contact, while 4 inches can be pierced by contact at a 60-degree angle.

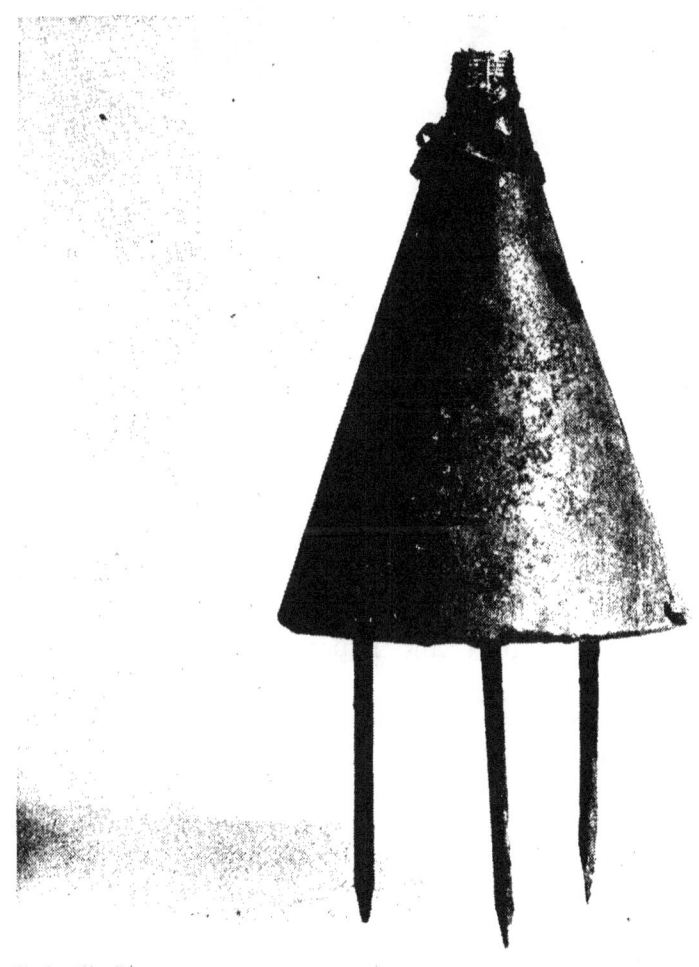

Figure 180.—Lunge antitank mine without pole attached.

Concrete Mine

This mine consists of a 19- by 9- by 8-inch concrete block enclosing a quart-size bottle filled with black powder. An iron carrying handle is fixed on one side. The mine weighs 40 pounds and is fired electrically.

Figure 181.— Concrete mine.

Sack-type Mine

This improvised mine is made by placing TNT in a canvas bag about the size of a seat cushion. The fuze assembly is made by putting together a Type 1 (1941) fuze igniter and Types 1 (1941) and 97 (1937) detonating caps.

The mine is used to destroy tanks at close range. Although designed to be hand-thrown on top of tanks, if the time fuze is set to go off in 1 or 2 seconds, it will still be effective should it fall under the tank. For use against heavy or medium tanks, 7 to 10 kilograms (15.4 to 22 pounds) of powder are used; for use against light amphibious tanks 5 kilograms (11 pounds) are sufficient.

Figure 182.—Sack-type mine.

4-Kilogram Improvised Shaped-Charge Mine

This mine is a wooden box, with inside dimensions of 8.27 by 8.27 by 3.15 inches, filled with 4 kilograms (8.8 pounds) of Type 97 (1937) picric acid blocks forming a cone to give the shaped-charge effect.

It is used for destroying tracks and penetrating armor of parked or slow-moving tanks. When used as a laid mine, it is placed directly on top of a Type 93 tape-measure mine to increase its effectiveness. It is also used as an electrical remote control mine. The blast will penetrate 2.36 inches of armor, and is effective against all parts of light and amphibious tanks; the underside, rear, and upper body of medium tanks; and the tracks of heavy tanks.

6-Kilogram Improvised Shaped-Charge Mine

This mine is constructed in the same manner as the 4-kilogram, except for the use of 6 kilograms (13.2 pounds) of Karitto explosive in place of picric acid, and the inside dimensions are 10 by 10 by 6.12 inches. Operation and effectiveness are the same as those of the 4-kilogram charge.

8-Kilogram Improvised Shaped-Charge Mine

This mine, constructed in the same manner as the 4- and 6-kilogram charges, contains 8 kilograms (17.6 pounds) of Karitto explosive. Inside dimensions are 11.02 by 11.02 by 6.15 inches. The mine is always laid with the base of the cone facing up, and is generally fired by electrical remote control. Its blast will penetrate 2.75 inches of armor.

Type 3 (1943) Conical Hand-Thrown Mine

This hand-thrown mine consists of a bowl-shaped wooden base, 2.75 inches in diameter, connected by an explosive-filled truncated cone to a "Universal"-type fuze assembly. A 10-inch long tail of hemp-palm fibers or grass is attached to the igniter at the upper end of the mine to afford greater accuracy in throwing, and to cause the mine to strike base-first. The explosive, weighing 17.6 ounces, consists of TNT, cyclonite, and tetryl. In the center of the explosive cone is a hollow portion lined with a funnel-shaped sheet of aluminum.

The Japanese claim that this mine, when thrown against the side of a tank, will penetrate 2.75 inches of armor. The "Universal"-type fuze will function regardless of the angle at which the mine strikes the tank. When it hits with the cone base-first, inertia causes the firing pin to travel forward against the action of the firing-pin spring, striking the percussion cap which in turn sets off the charge.

Figure 183.— Type 3 (1943) conical hand-thrown mine, large size.

Figure 184.— Type 3 (1943) conical hand-thrown mine, small size.

Figure 185.—Fuze for Type 3 (1943) conical hand-thrown mine, large size.

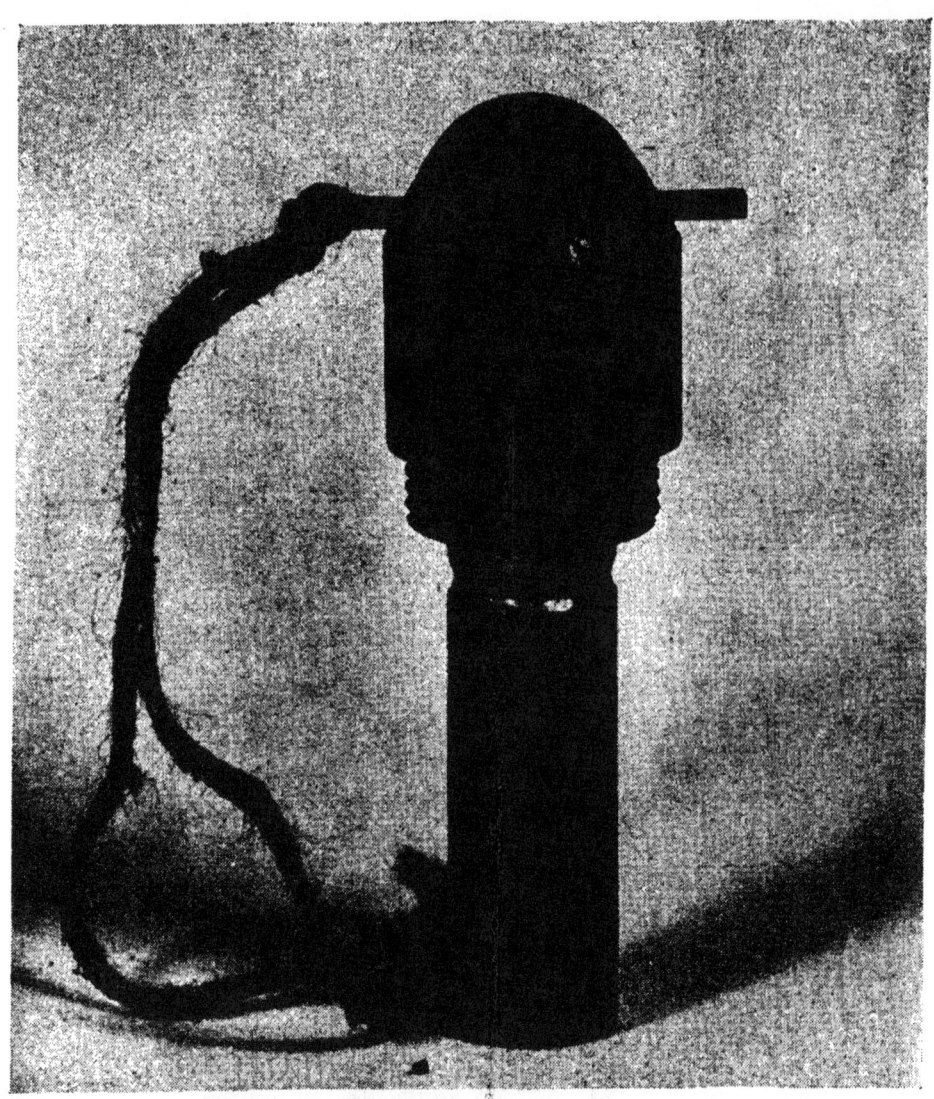

Figure 186.— Fuze for Type 3 (1943) conical hand-thrown mine, small size.

Coconut Land Mine

This field-expedient mine utilizes the shell of a coconut and a Type 91 (1931) hand grenade. The coconut is hollowed out and stuffed with plain black powder. The grenade is fitted in so that its top is flush with the top of the coconut and its cap protrudes. The whole assembly is bound with chicken wire to hold the grenade in place and to provide a carrying handle.

SPECIFICATIONS:

Weight of mine	6 to 7 pounds.
Type of explosive	Black powder.
Weight of explosive	24 to 34 ounces.

In an antipersonnel use, fragmentation is ample within an estimated radius of 10 to 20 yards. Although less effective than the Type 93 or Type 99 mines, it is probably capable of damaging small vehicles.

Figure 187.— Coconut mine.

Experimental Hand-Thrown Mine

This mine consists of a spherical, aluminum main body, a bursting charge, and a fuze. The explosive charge consists of a mixture of TNT, cyclonite, and tetryl. The fuze, a "Universal" instantaneous type, consists of the body, striker, hammer, detonator chamber, spring detonator, and striking pin.

SPECIFICATIONS:

Diameter	**4.7 inches.**
Height plus fuze and protective cap	**5.4 inches.**
Weight	**3.5 pounds.**
Weight of filling	**3.0 pounds.**

Naval Depth Charge Improvised Mine

This Japanese depth charge, which contains 250 pounds of explosive, is 30 inches long and 18 inches in diameter, and resembles an ash can. A well, or tube, set in one end of the charge, holds a booster, a detonating cap, and a simple striker pin. There is no safety pin or retaining spring to hold the striker immobile. This mine has been found buried with an improvised pressure plate in contact with the firing mechanism. The pressure plate consisted of a board cover, to the center of which a short wooden post was attached at right angles. This post acts as a plunger against the striker.

Figure 188.— Type 2 (1942) naval depth charge.

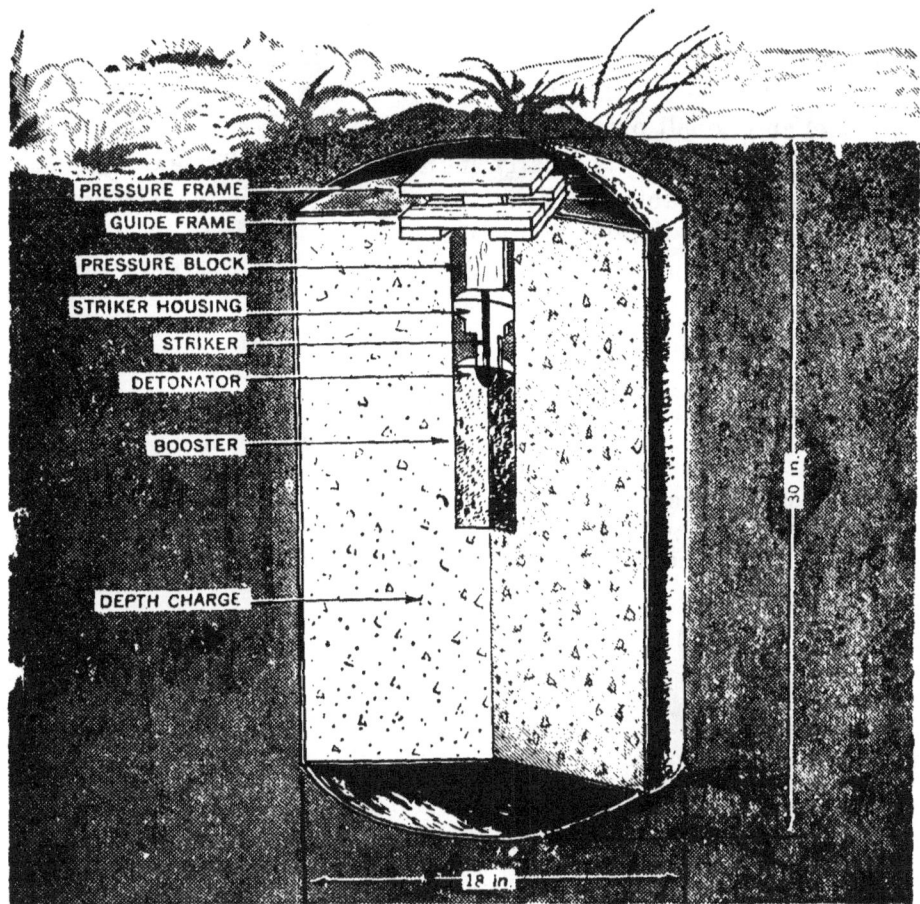

Figure 189.— Type 2 (1942) naval depth charge as used as improvised mine.

Pole Charge

This charge usually consists of a Type 93 antitank mine fastened to a long bamboo pole, but cases have been reported where improvised containers, filled with high explosive and equipped with a pull-type igniter, have been affixed to poles.

The charge is used by infiltrating Japanese troops along tank approaches. The individual attacker hides until a tank arrives opposite his position at which time he rushes from cover to push the charge under the tank tracks.

Type 99 (1939) Magnetic Demolition Charge

This magnetic charge consists of eight separate sections of cast TNT, assembled to form a circular disc held together by a khaki canvas cover.

Four magnets are attached to the cover at right angles to each other by a strong canvas ribbon sewn to the cover. Each magnet consists of an aluminum box, containing a permanent magnet cone of a compact, black, friable powder which is a light mixture of sintered iron, and nickel and cobalt oxides. Two soft iron plates act as pole pieces, and respective polarity is clearly indicated by the letters N and S. The magnet is capable of lifting 6.5 pounds of iron. The igniter recess, which runs diametrically through three of the sections, is filled before use by a wooden plug 3.75 inches long.

SPECIFICATIONS OF CHARGE:

Diameter (without magnets)	4.75 inches.
Thickness	1.50 inches.
Weight with fuze	2 pounds, 7 ounces.
Weight (plugged)	2 pounds, 7 ounces.
Type of explosive	Cast TNT.
Weight of explosive	1 pound, 10 ounces.
Dimensions of magnets	1.5 by 1.25 by 0.75 inch.
Weight of each magnet	3 ounces.

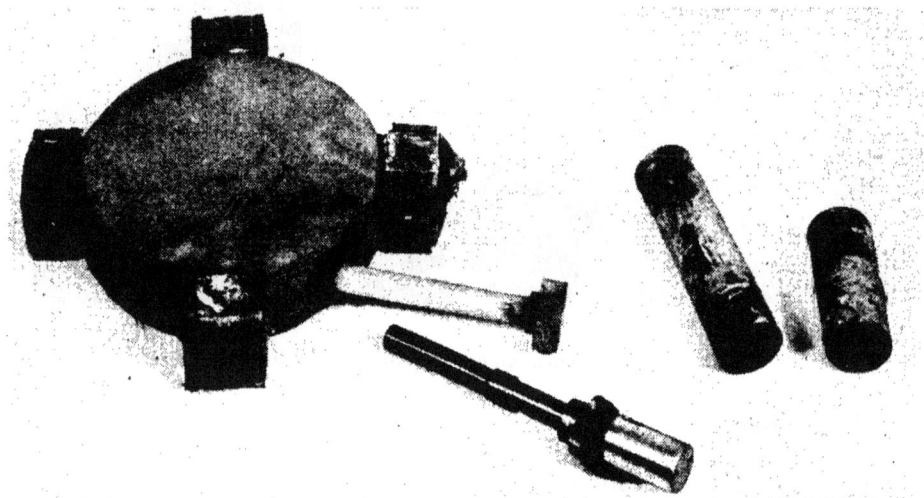

Figure 190.— Type 99 (1939) magnetic demolition charge.

Fuze

This consists of three distinct portions: the striker mechanism; the percussion cap and powder delay train in the middle tube, which also carries the threaded brass locking ring for screwing the fuze into the charge; and the detonator, screwed over the middle tube. It is 0.60 inch in diameter (at head), weighs 4 ounces, and has a delay of 4 to 5 seconds.

When the safety pin is withdrawn, a sharp hit on the fuze cap will overcome the compression spring and press the fuze cap into a position where the four steel balls can escape into the ring groove. This releases the striker spring and fires the percussion cap which ignites the powder delay train, and so the detonator and main charge. After insertion of the safety pin or wire into the safety pin hole, neutralization is completed by unscrewing the locking ring and withdrawing the fuze.

With the fuze screwed into place and the safety pin withdrawn, the charge must be placed by hand in direct contact with any flat steel or iron surface of the target. The delay after hitting the fuze cap should be 5 to 6 seconds, but anything from 4 to 10 seconds has been reported. The penetration effect against steel armor plate is 0.75 inch for a single charge, and about 1.25 inches for two charges placed one above the other.

Suction-Cup Mine

This mine, somewhat similar in appearance to the Japanese lunge mine, is attached to the target by two suction cups. Its charge is initiated by means of pull igniters with a delay of about 10 seconds. The mine body is a black, cylindrical sheet-metal container closed at both ends and filled with explosive. A hole in the top cover of the container permits two large blasting caps to be inserted into a pocket in the explosive charge. A broomstick-size handle is fitted into metal seating on the top of the container. Two powerful rubber suction cups are attached near the base of the charge container by two metal loops.

Two friction igniters are tied to the upper end of the handle. A short delay is provided by two 4.25-inch lengths of safety fuze, extending from the igniters to two blasting caps. The caps are lashed to two lengths of primacord, which runs the length of the handle and are crimped to two more blasting caps that fit into the pocket in the top of the main charge.

SPECIFICATIONS:
Total length	5 feet, 6 inches.
Diameter of mine body	4.187 inches.
Length of mine body	5.312 inches.
Weight of explosive	4 pounds, 7.5 ounces.
Type of explosive	TNT, 53 percent.
	RDX, 47 percent.
Diameter of suction cups	3.25 inches.

When the mine is placed against the target, the friction igniters are pulled, starting the safety fuze burning. At the end of a 10- to 18-second delay, the blasting caps set off the primacord which instantaneously sets off the two blasting caps in the explosive charge. If only half of the handle is used, the primacord and its blasting caps may be omitted; the blasting caps attached to the safety fuze then may be placed directly into the main charge.

Tool-Box Mine

This mine, as its name implies, resembles a metal tool box in appearance. It consists of a rectangular box filled with explosive. Standard fuzes for the Type 93 (tape-measure) mine are set in two holes, prepared by cutting through the metal case and making wells in the explosive to receive the igniters.

SPECIFICATIONS:
- Length of box _____ 20.75 inches.
- Width of box _____ 5.562 inches.
- Height of box _____ 4.312 inches.
- Total weight _____ 33 pounds (approx.)
- Weight of explosive _____ 32.5 pounds (approx.).

Operation is the same as for the tape-measure mine.

Mouse-Trap Mine

This is an improvised, spring-loaded, all-purpose, detonating mechanism not unlike a mouse trap in general appearance. It is composed of a cylindrical pointed firing pin, wired to a wooden block in such a manner that it can be set and tripped in the manner of a mouse trap. The striker is tensioned by a coiled spring. This spring is compressed when the mechanism is set, and the slightest touch or movement will release the firing pin. The wooden block to which the firing pin is wired has a small cavity into which a blasting cap fits. The main explosive charge can be any bulk explosive or any other standard demolition charge.

Rifle Grenades

Type 2 (1942) 40-mm Hollow-Charge Rifle Grenade

This antitank rifle grenade, a copy of the German *Gewehr Panzergranate*, is fired from a cup-type, rifled launcher using a special crimped blank cartridge. It is believed that it is used with both 6.5-mm and 7.7-mm rifles.

The upper body, fitted with a hollow nose cap, contains TNT cast around the usual shaped cone. The lower cylindrical body (tail) is pre-rifled for engagement in the rifling of the launcher, and contains a base detonating fuze, which is armed by setback action on firing and detonates on impact.

The launcher, which is believed to be used with both 6.5-mm and 7.7-mm rifles, is a copy of the German *Schiessbecher*. A hinged clamp fastens the base of the launcher behind the front sight of the rifle. For firing, the tail of the grenade is twisted into the rifled launcher. Rotation of the grenade stabilizes it in flight and assures base detonation.

The grenade is fired by means of a crimped blank cartridge.

SPECIFICATIONS:

Length over-all	7.1 inches.
Length of upper body	4.2 inches.
Diameter of upper body	1.6 inches.
Length of lower body	2.9 inches.
Diameter of lower body	1.2 inches.
Weight	13.0 ounces.
Type of filling	TNT, 50 percent. Cyclonite, 50 percent.
Weight of filling	3.5 ounces.
Type of fuze	Base detonating.
Time delay	None.
Penetration	3.88 inches mild steel by static test.

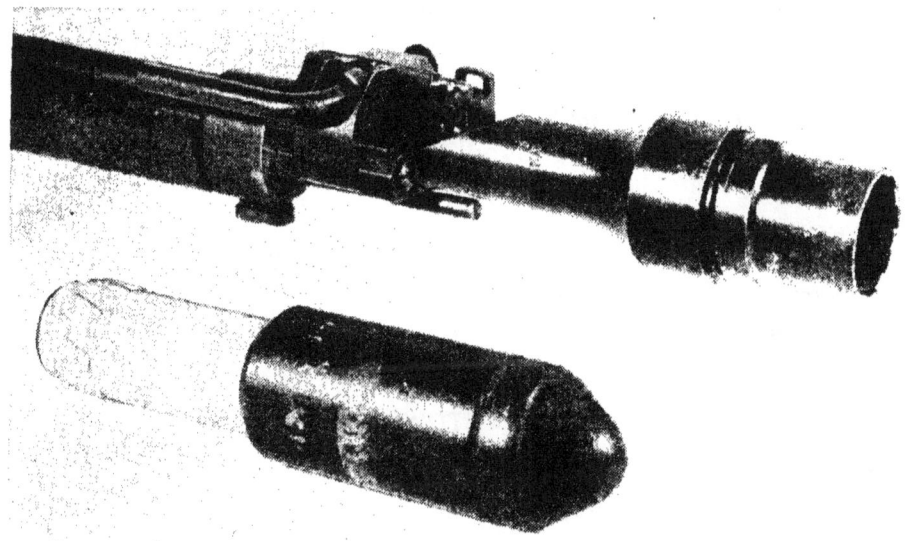

Figure 191.— Type 2 (1942) 40-mm hollow-charge rifle grenade.

Type 2 (1942) 30-mm Hollow-Charge Rifle Grenade

This antitank rifle grenade uses the same launcher and is a smaller version of the 40-mm Type 2 grenade.

SPECIFICATIONS:

Length over-all	6.4 inches.
Length of upper body	3.8 inches.
Length of lower body	2.9 inches.

Diameter of upper body	1.2 inches.
Weight	8.1 ounces.
Type of filling	{TNT, 50 percent. Cyclonite, 50 percent.
Weight of filling	1.76 ounces.

Figure 192.— Type 2 (1942) 30-mm hollow charge rifle grenade.

Flame Throwers

Type 93 (1933) Flame Thrower

The fuel unit of this flame thrower comprises two fuel tanks and a pressure cylinder. Ignition of the fuel jet is effected by flash from a blank cartridge, ten of which are loaded in the revolving cylinder located at the nozzle of the flame gun. The firing mechanism is actuated by an operating handle which controls the fuel ejection valve.

SPECIFICATIONS:
Maximum range	25 to 30 yards.
Duration of continuous discharge	10 to 12 seconds.
Fuel capacity	—3.25 gallons.
Total weight, charged	55 pounds (approx.).

Type 100 (1940) Flame Thrower

The fuel unit of this type is identical with the Type 93, as are range and duration of flame. The differences in the flame guns are tabulated below.

	Type 93	Type 100
Over-all length	47.125 inches	35.5 inches.
Weight	10 pounds	8.5 pounds.
Nozzle outlet tip	Fixed	Removable.

Flame-thrower accessories include Type 99 (1939) small air compressor, used to recharge the pressure cylinder of Type 93 and Type 100 flame throwers. The gasoline-engine driven compressor is packed in a wooden carrying case, 18 inches square and 13.5 inches high.

CHAPTER V. Antitank Methods

General Doctrine

The Japanese, in a full realization of the effectiveness of Allied armor, have overlooked few of the usual methods of antitank warfare in their efforts to counterbalance Allied superiority in tank operations. Normal antitank weapons have been supplemented by antitank ditches and barricades as well as by mines and other types of explosives. Nevertheless, Japanese antitank units still appear to be handicapped by both the limited capabilities and the insufficient number of their antitank weapons.

In an effort to compensate for these deficiencies, the Japanese have organized and trained a variety of assault teams, which launch attacks at close quarters upon the most vulnerable points of tanks. These teams are armed with whatever weapons and explosive charges are available, and their equipment may include items from an extraordinary series of hand-carried demolition weapons. Many of the missions of these close-combat units are more hazardous than our doctrine would advocate, since the majority of such attacks result in the death of tank hunters.

Although the effectiveness of these improvised antitank tactics is limited, a fairly complete system of antimechanized defenses is obtained when the special-assault-team attacks are combined with the more common antitank operations, and when the enemy's support of his tanks has been overcome.

Employment of Antitank Guns

Each Japanese infantry regiment has at least four and sometimes six antitank guns. These are 37-mm or 47-mm weapons. The most effective antitank gun in the Japanese Army is the Type 1 (1941) 47-mm weapon which appears gradually to be replacing the older 37-mm gun. These guns are assigned as organic weapons of the regimental antitank-gun company. In some Japanese infantry divisions and brigades encountered in the Central Pacific, however, the antitank guns have been allocated to battalions, and are the armament of one platoon of the battalion gun company.

Some of these units already mentioned, and other infantry units, may include one or two automatic guns, generally the Type 97 (1937) 20-mm weapon, in the machine-gun company or the machine-gun platoons, if these platoons are organic within the rifle company. In the Japanese armored division two antitank guns are included in the armament of the rifle company of the mobile infantry regiment, in addition to the 18 guns of the division antitank battalion.

Reinforcement of the antitank defenses is furnished by independent antitank units, both battalions and companies, which may be attached to divisions and smaller units for direct support of operations against tanks. The independent battalion consists of three companies, each with four, sometimes six, 37-mm or 47-mm antitank guns. The independent company has eight 37-mm or 47-mm antitank guns.

In action, the firing unit is the individual gun, and the gun commander selects the most suitable target and opens fire on his own initiative. If the terrain permits, the antitank gunner holds his fire until the range is overwhelmingly favorable to him, often waiting until a tank approaches within 50 yards or less. Several guns may operate as a team, and coordination may be effected among gun teams, special-assault teams or tank hunters, and supporting infantry. One instance of close cooperation between antitank artillery and suicide tank hunters occurred in the Philippines. The advance of a column of three Allied tanks was halted when the Japanese scored a direct hit on the leading tank with a 47-mm antitank gun. Immediately 15 to 20 Japanese armed with satchel charges and incendiary grenades swarmed around the tanks. While the two squads of supporting Allied infantry were pinned down by fire from a Japanese machine gun, the Japanese succeeded in setting fire to two tanks and blowing a tread off the third.

Each Japanese gun normally will have 60 to 100 rounds of HE and AP ammunition at the gun position. The ammunition platoon replenishes the supply of each gun squad from the company dump, which in turn draws from the battalion dump. Supply generally follows a route from larger to smaller units, with the larger unit furnishing both manpower and transportation.

Selection of Positions

In normal land operations, some guns are placed as far forward as possible, with a number of weapons held in a more rearward position, both as a reserve and to give the defense as much depth as terrain and situation permit. Concealment and camouflage of positions are stressed. Alternate positions are prepared so that guns can be moved frequently. Guns are sited where they can best cover logical avenues of approach, and occasionally an infantry unit may be attached for local protection. Positions are selected where advantage can be taken of natural obstacles, and artifical obstacles are constructed whenever and wherever possible. Flanking fire is customary.

In addition, antitank guns may be sited in positions on steep ridges or rocky slopes from which they can open fire while remaining relatively inaccessible to the tanks and supporting infantry. When the Japanese place antitank guns in areas affording heavy cover, they may cut small fire tunnels in the vegetation in the same manner as they do for machine guns.

Artillery pieces of larger caliber than the 47-mm gun have been used by the Japanese to counter tank attacks. The 70-mm battalion howitzer and the 75-mm regimental gun have been employed to cover road blocks, antitank obstacles, and minefields. In one phase of the campaign in Burma, the Japanese employed nearly all of their field artillery exclusively against tanks and tank-infantry attacks. In one town in Burma, the bulk of the Japanese artillery was sited to bring direct fire on tanks whose routes of approach were confined to the city streets.

Large-Scale Antitank Defense

To combat tanks on a large scale, the Japanese have devised what they call an "elastic defense" (*dansei bogyo*). At the approach of a tank attack in force, only about 20 percent of available heavy infantry weapons are fired from front-line positions. With the exception of one squad per platoon, all units fall back 800 to 1,500 yards. The squads remaining on the front line scatter, lay a smoke screen, and attack the tanks with incendiary grenades as they come through the smoke. While the tanks are meeting this resistance, they come under the fire of all the main Japanese antitank weapons, sited 500 to 600 yards to the rear. Meanwhile, the division artillery moves forward to positions which permit direct firing on the tanks, thus supporting the infantry either in defense or in counterattack.

Japanese sources state that once a tank attack is stopped by this "elastic defense" method, the hostile forces are to be pinched off. The Japanese infantry, although scattered, can still offer successful opposition to hostile infantry which might attempt to exploit the advance of tanks. This large-scale antitank defense does not however, seem to have been used extensively in the field.

Tank Hunters

The Japanese, unable to cope successfully with Allied armor by conventional methods of antitank defense, have put unusual stress on close-quarter attacks. Individuals or small groups making these attacks are known as "tank hunters," and their desperate, often suicidal, measures have received increased emphasis in recent operations.

Tank-hunter teams are organized and trained to attack tanks in battle at their vulnerable points, or to infiltrate into tank parks as small raiding parties to destroy the vehicles there. Each Japanese infantry platoon may have one of these units armed with demolition equipment, incendiaries, armor-piercing mines, mines tied to grenades, clusters of grenades, Molotov cocktails, or pole mines. Frequently, a group will operate with a combination of these weapons.

Where tanks move slowly because of terrain difficulties, they can be more easily approached and attacked by these tank-hunter teams, particularly if supporting infantry fails to keep up with the advancing tanks. Because it is difficult to assault a tank moving faster than 10 miles an hour, tank-hunter teams are taught to select as ambush points defiles, narrow roads, fords, or rough trails through dense vegetation. They are quick to attack tanks that have outdistanced their infantry support, or that have been immobilized or forced to slow down by antitank obstacles, terrain, or damage. Attacks at dawn, at dusk, or in rainy weather are preferred, but the tank hunters will attack at any opportune time.

The assault teams often concentrate on command tanks, but they may attack several tanks simultaneously. In any case, they are taught to direct their attacks against the most vulnerable points, including treads, air vents and other points on the rear of tanks, observation ports and periscopes at the front, the turret and turret ring, and the tank weapons and gun mantlet.

Methods of Attack

In assaulting a tank, each member of the tank-hunter team has a specific mission. One man tries to throw an antitank mine or demolition charge under the track tread, or to place it there by hand or on the end of a pole. A second member of the team may throw a Molotov cocktail or some other incendiary to force the crew to abandon the tank. If these efforts fail, the assault team may try to mount the tank and force the ports with small-arms fire and grenades. When attacking a light tank, the Japanese may try to halt it by jamming a pole into the treads, near the driving wheels, and then cripple it with

Figure 193.—Type of tank-hunting unit.

picks and crowbars. Smoke grenades or candles may be used in an effort to blind the tank crew, to force them out of the tank, or to hide the tank from its infantry support.

The Japanese may adopt deceptive measures to approach the tank without arousing suspicion. In one instance, a Japanese, dressed in an American uniform, climbed upon a tank and dropped a grenade inside it. In another instance, eight to ten Japanese, holding a conversation in English, strolled casually into a tank park chatting about racing at Santa Anita. They fled as soon as their deception was discovered, leaving behind several shell cases filled with explosives, with detonators attached.

Japanese sources indicate another method in which a group of three tank hunters (designated "group leader," "No. 1," and "No. 2") might operate. Number 1 hurls a Molotov cocktail, and if the weapon strikes the tank he yells "a hit." In that case the others do not attack. If the throw is unsuccessful, Number 1 will call out "miss," whereupon the group leader, using a pole charge, attempts to damage the tracks and thus stop the tank. Number 2, before the explosion of the pole charges, seeks to destroy or damage the tank's guns by placing an adhesive mine or some similar explosive under them. The Japanese recommend that Number 2 attack the tank simultaneously with the leader if the former is armed with an armor-piercing mine. Otherwise he awaits the result of the leader's effort.

A two-man group, according to Japanese sources, includes the leader, carrying a pole mine, and Number 1, carrying a Molotov cocktail. The tank is attacked simultaneously from both sides as it enters terrain favorable to the tank hunters.

According to a prisoner of war, an independent antitank company was organized on Okinawa from line-of-communication troops. The company had a strength of about 100 men and was considered to be a suicide unit. The troops, armed only with satchel charges, were expected to infiltrate into Allied lines or to remain in covered positions, waiting to make an attack when it would be most unexpected. Also, certain men in each platoon of every rifle company were designated to carry out this same duty.

Combat Unit Teams

According to instructions issued by the Japanese for attacking tanks with explosives, close-quarter combat units used against tanks are composed mainly of infantry and engineer troops. These combat unit teams are divided into several land-mine squads (firing squads), destruction squads, a reserve squad, and, where necessary, a covering squad. Each team is assigned the task of destroying one tank.

The land-mine squad consists of ten men with a noncommissioned officer as leader. The first duty of this squad is to plant mines along the possible avenues of tank approach. One man in each squad is designated as the "igniter"; presumably his responsibility is to explode controlled mines at the proper moment. After mines are planted, the land-mine squad's next duty is to act as a fire squad and to create opportunities for the destruction squad by means of machine-gun and rifle fire designed to separate the hostile covering infantry from the tanks they are supporting. To accomplish this mission, the squad is equipped with two or three light machine guns.

The destruction squad is composed of several men with a noncommissioned officer as leader. It attempts to destroy the hostile tank, using mines and explosives which its members throw or place against the tank.

As soon as the hostile tanks and their covering infantry approach the mined areas, each team is assigned a tank. The emplaced land mines are detonated by the igniter; and the land-mine (fire) squad opens fire on the Allied infantry and any exposed tank crew. The destruction squad, which has been waiting nearby, makes close-quarter attacks on the chosen tank. Smoke may be used to isolate the tank and cover the attackers.

The reserve squad performs, when necessary, the duties of either the land-mine or destruction squads. The covering squad, in addition to covering the activities of the land-mine and destruction squads, also furnishes covering fire during the withdrawal of the other elements of the close-quarter combat unit when the tank-destroying mission has been completed.

Tankborne Infantry

One type of tank fighter that appears to be scheduled for much greater use by the Japanese is the tankborne infantryman. Three to seven of these men ride on a light tank, and four to eight are carried by a medium tank. When advancing against hostile fire, the tankborne infantrymen lie flat on the tank, and may return the fire if possible. Also, if engaged in close combat, or upon receiving fire from snipers, they fire from the tank or attempt to use hand grenades. The infantrymen usually dismount on orders from the tank commander, but exercise their own initiative in this respect if close individual combat is expected or minefields are encountered.

After the tankborne infantrymen have dismounted they and the tank crew endeavor to operate as a unit. The infantry furnishes close support by advancing with or ahead of the tank. In return, the tank attempts to support the movement of the infantry. When hostile tanks are encountered, the Japanese infantry attempts to take advantage of friendly tank fire to engage in individual combat against these tanks, as well as against tanks that may approach from the rear or flanks.

Japanese tankborne infantry is also expected to neutralize antitank weapons carried by opposing infantry and to clear minefields. In addition, it assists in laying smoke screens, short-range reconnaissance, guiding, routing, observation, and command liaison. The organization of a four- to six-man tankborne-infantry assault unit and the antitank weapons to be used are shown in Figure 194.

Number of Men	Team Member	Duty	Material Carried	Weapons Carried
4 Men	1	Leader	Axe, pick	One frangible smoke grenade, one Type 3 hand-thrown mine, one stick mine.
	2		Saw, shovel	Same, plus one smoke candle, one hydrocyanic-acid frangible grenade.
	3		Same as above	Same.
	4		Same as above	Same, plus one stick mine.
5 Men	1	Leader	Saw, pick	One frangible smoke grenade, one Type 3 hand-thrown mine, one stick mine.
	2		Saw, shovel	Same, plus one smoke candle, one hydrocyanic-acid frangible grenade.
	3		Same as above	Same.
	4		Same as above	Same, plus one stick mine.
	5		Same as above	Same.
6 Men	1	Leader	Axe, pick	One frangible smoke grenade, one Type 3 hand-thrown mine, one stick mine.
	2		Saw, shovel	Same, plus one smoke candle, one hydrocyanic-acid frangible grenade.
	3		Same as above	Same.
	4		Axe, pick	Same, plus one stick mine.
	5		Shovel	Same.
	6		Same as above	Same.
Remarks	The tank is equipped with the following weapons: Five frangible smoke grenades, ten Type 3 hand-thrown mines, ten smoke candles, five stick land mines, two hydrocyanic-acid frangible grenades.			

Figure 194.—Organization of a tankborne infantry assault unit.

Figure 195.—Frangible smoke grenade (right); and carrying case (left).

Figure 196.—Hydrocyanic acid frangible grenade.

Figure 197.—Molotov cocktail.

Instructions issued by a Japanese infantry division headquarters contemplated the use of the motorized company of the division reconnaissance regiment in antitank combat. The instructions stressed thorough training in individual suicide attacks against hostile tanks, with 5 to 10 kilograms (11 to 22 pounds) of explosive to be used, probably by each man. Figures 198 to 206 illustrate the tactical formations to be used by the motorized company in the attack against tanks.

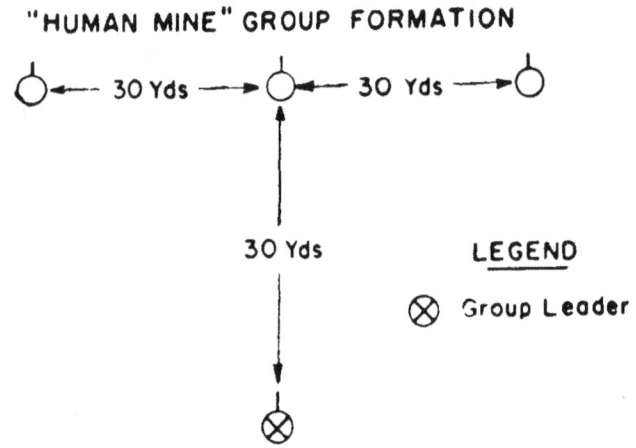

Figure 198.

The Japanese have made extensive use of snipers in their assaults on Allied armor. The snipers are employed to break up the infantry-tank attack in the early stages by sniping at tank commanders or by attempting to separate the tanks from their supporting infantry.

Engineer Assault Team

Instructions issued by the Japanese Army Engineer School describe the tactics of another type of assault team. In an attack by this team, smoke is used to neutralize the opposing tanks. The attack is preceded by the throwing of smoke candles and grenades. In addition, an artillery smoke screen is laid down.

Although organization depends upon the mission, the engineer assault team generally is divided into neutralization, track-destroying, and demolition sections, with a noncommissioned officer as leader. The neutralization section, composed of two or three men, constitutes the leading element of the assault team. It makes surprise attacks on tanks and creates an opportunity for the other sections to engage

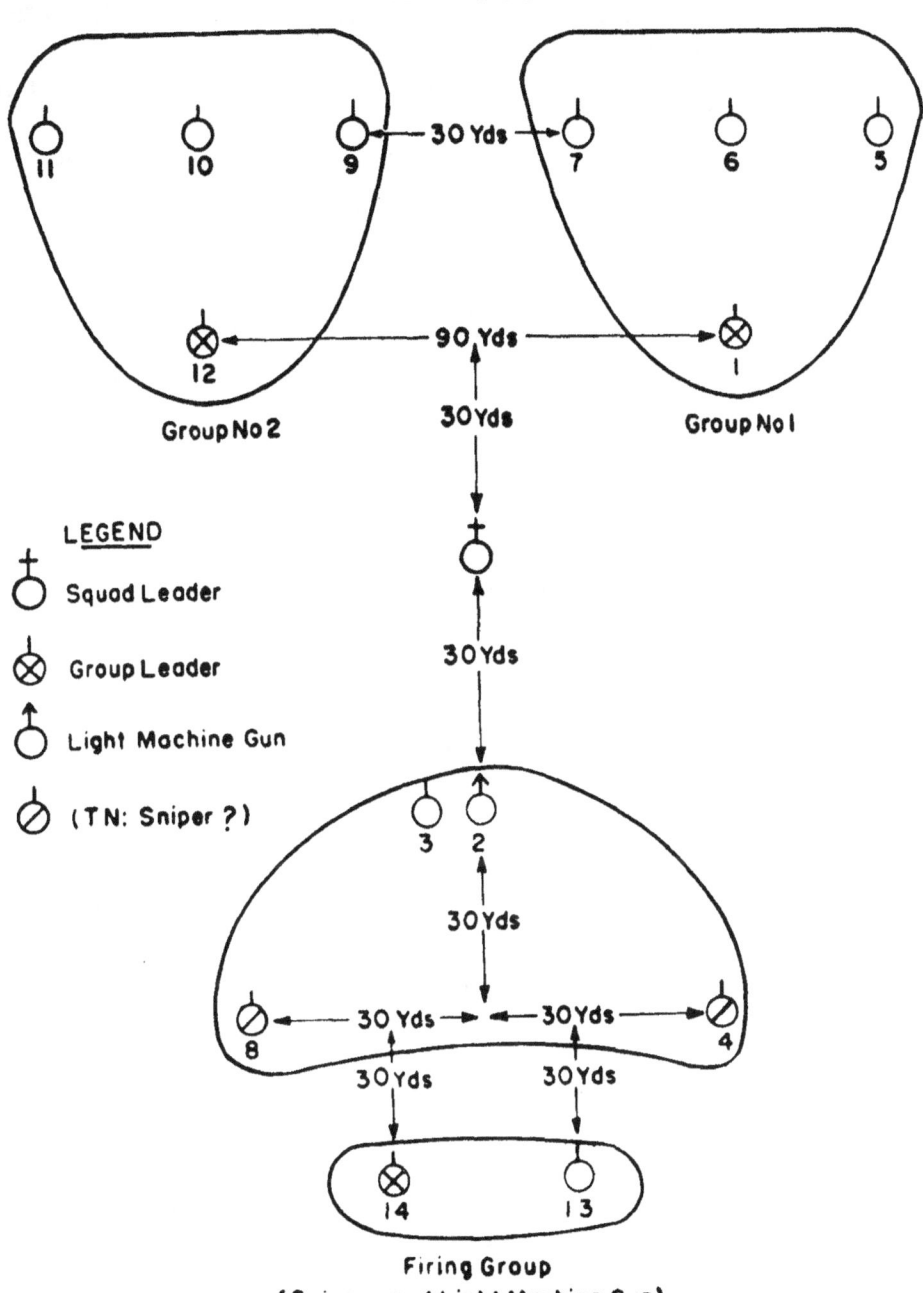

Figure 199.

in close combat. When the tank has been neutralized, the track-destroying section, also composed of two or three men, assaults the tank, usually only on one side, and attempts to destroy the tracks. The demolition section, of two or three men, takes advantage of the destructive work of the track-destroying section to administer the final blow by striking at the armor plates of the tank with armor-piercing explosives.

The assault team will usually attack one tank at a time, with particular attention to the lead or command tank. Several assault teams are deployed in depth in order to facilitate operations on successive tanks.

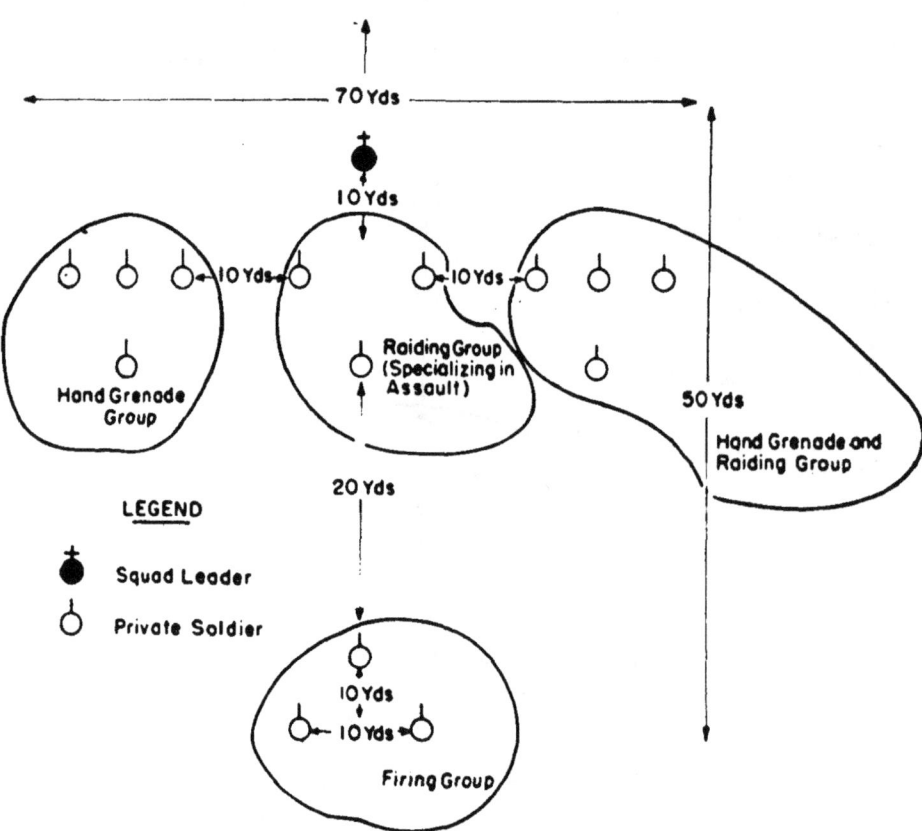

Figure 200.

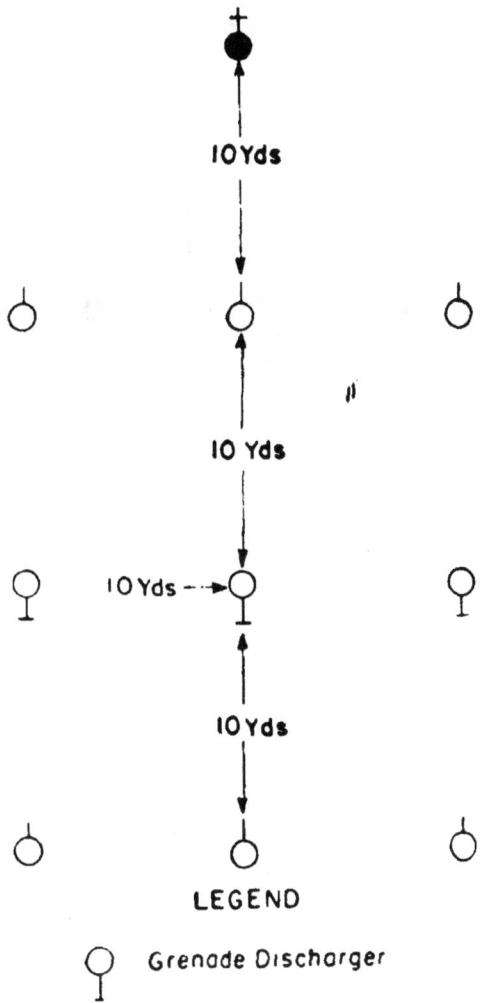

Figure 201.

187

PLATOON "HUMAN MINE" FORMATION
NUMBER ONE

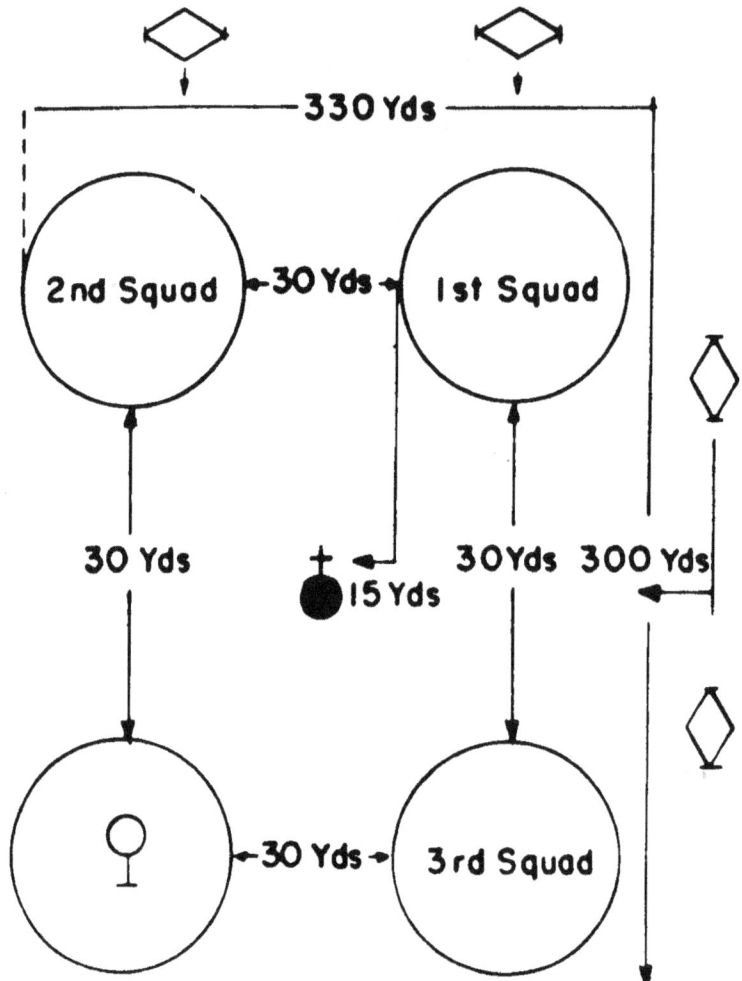

COMMAND. FORM No 1 CLOSE ASSAULT FORMATION
SIGNAL: RED AND WHITE FLAG, VERTICAL

LEGEND

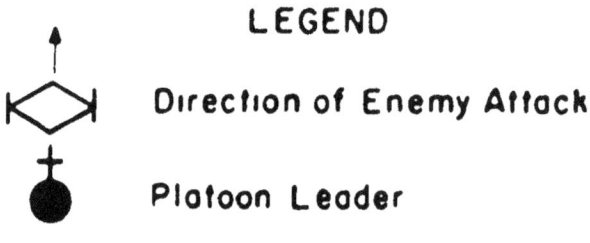

Figure 202.

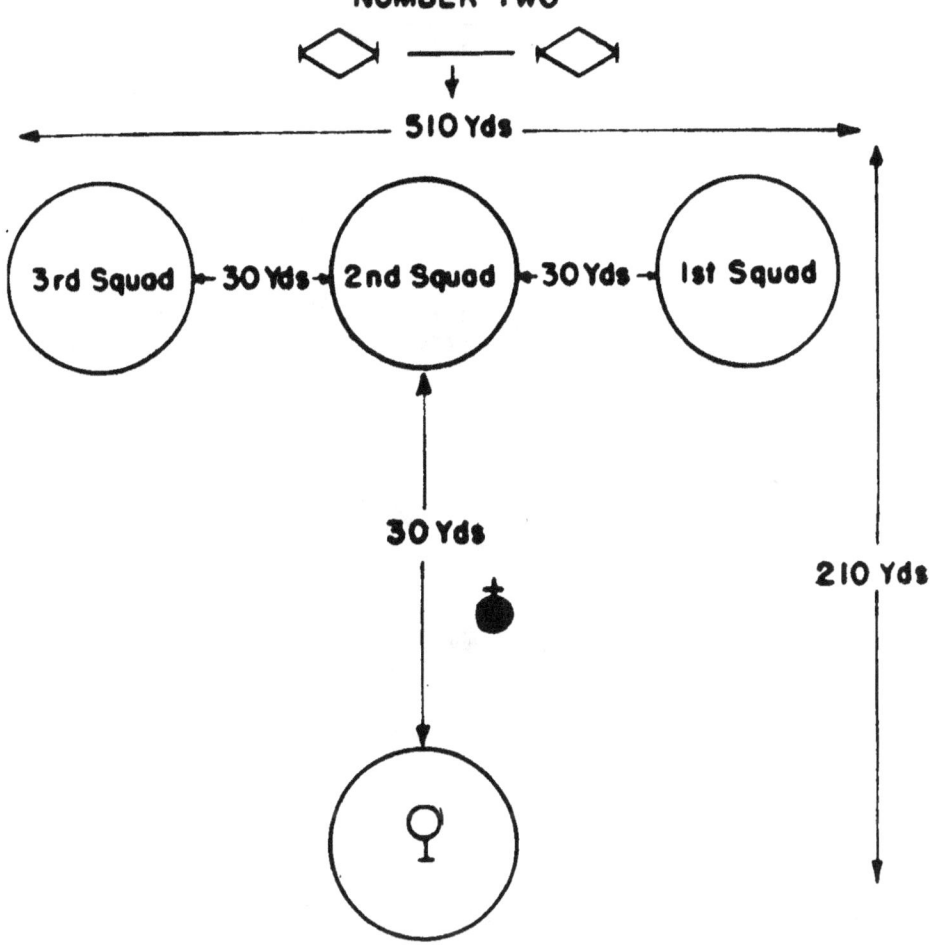

Figure 203.

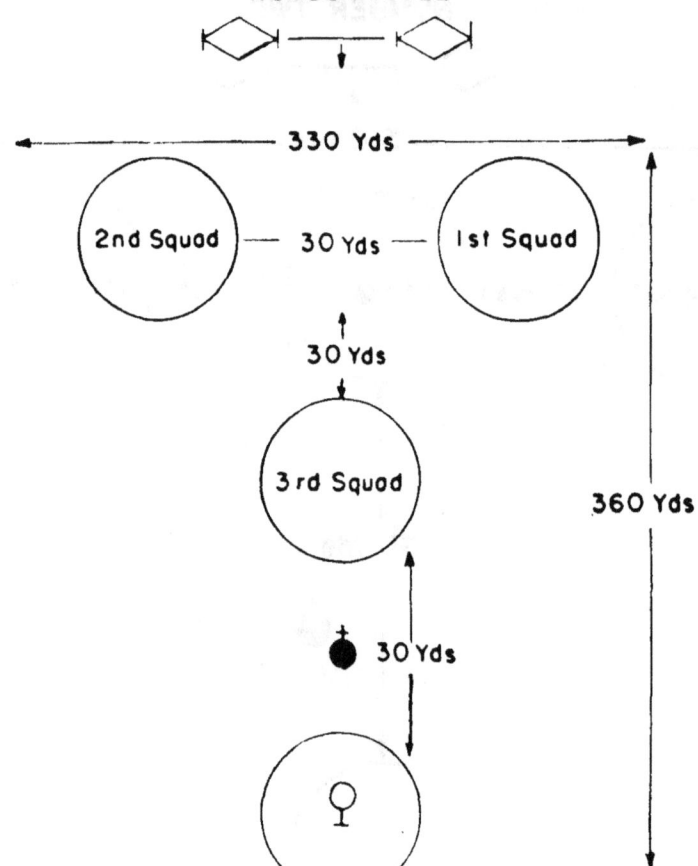

Figure 204.

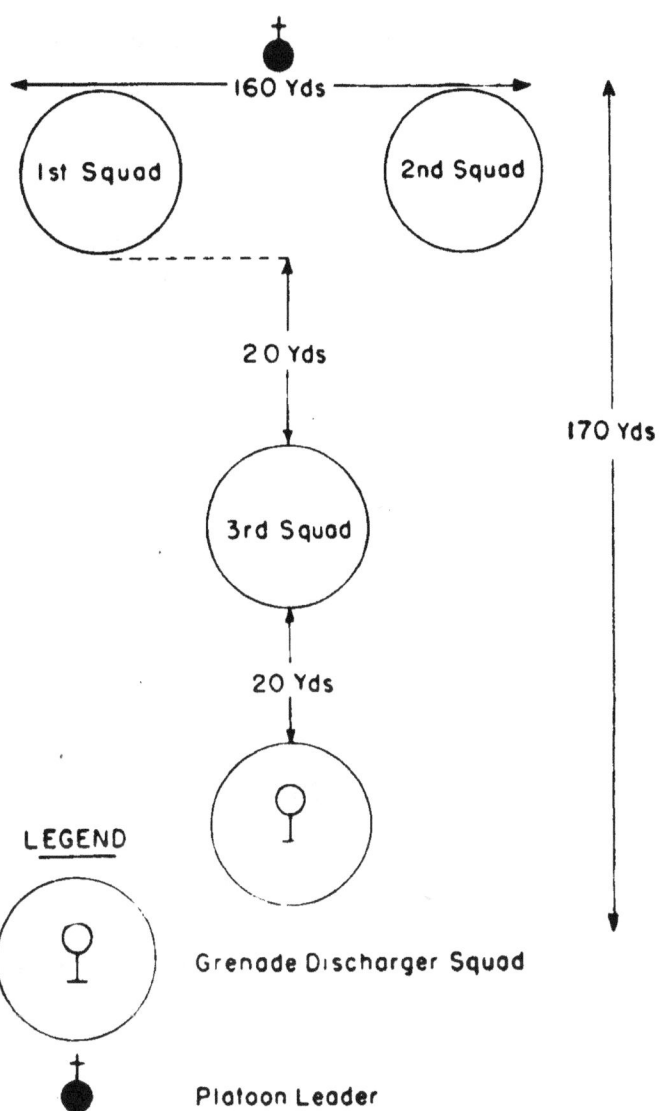

Figure 205.

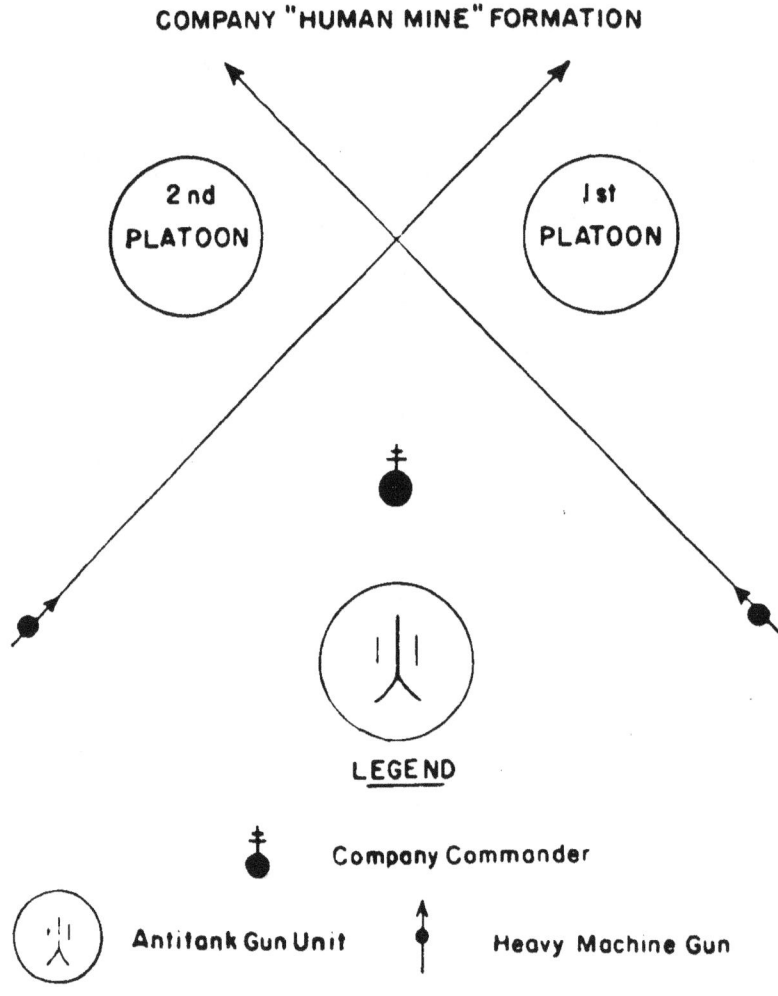

Figure 206.

If supporting Japanese infantry is attached to the assault team, the infantry attempts to isolate the tank under attack by its infantry support and then directs fire at the tank's observation ports.

The organization and disposition of an engineer assault team is shown in Figure 207.

Team Sections	Mission	Team Member	Portable Materials [1]
Leader	Command and attack preparations	------	One Type 3 hand-thrown mine. Two hand smoke candles.
Neutralization Section	a. Blinding with smoke attack b. Neutralizing the crew	1	Two hand smoke candles (smoke grenades). One smoke candle with attached cord.
		2	One Type 3 hand-thrown mine. One hand smoke candle (smoke grenade). One smoke candle with attached cord.
Track-Attack Section	Destroying track	3	Two Type 93 antitank mines. One mine on rod.
		4	Same as No. 3.
Demolition Section	a. Piercing armor plate b. Destroying engine c. Inflicting casualties	5	One 2-kilogram cone-shaped armor-piercing mine (rod attached).
		6	One 5-kilogram hemispherical armor-piercing mine (rod attached).

[1] Each individual will carry one hand grenade and one Type 99 magnetic demolition charge.

Figure 207.—An example of organization and disposition of an engineer assault team.

Assault Against Flame-Thrower Tanks

The Japanese concede that the psychological effect of the flame-thrower tank is greater than that of an ordinary tank. Accordingly, they stress that attacks against these tanks must be made with great vigor and daring. In the assault, effort is made to take advantage of the flame thrower's dead spaces, of lulls in operation, and of lack of visibility incident to flame emission. Often the Japanese will attempt, by deception, to cause a premature flame discharge and will hinder operation of both the flame thrower and the tank by the use of smoke. Flame-throwing tanks may also be neutralized by smoke candles fired from an improvised projector sited about 60 yards from the approaching tank.

The Japanese attack is often delivered simultaneously from several directions, or it may be delivered from the windward direction alone. Efforts may be made to destroy the fuel tanks and exposed exhaust pipe of the hostile tank. Special equipment for protection against the flames, including shields, gas masks, and gloves, may be used by the Japanese who also will take maximum advantage of natural terrain cover, trenches, and fox holes.

Individual Suicide Attacks

Japanese antitank methods include considerable individual action by Japanese soldiers in suicidal missions. In one instance, a Japanese soldier dug a well-camouflaged fox hole among the weeds just off the shoulder of a road barely two traffic lanes wide. A tape-measure mine was tied to the end of a 5-foot bamboo pole. Lying in the protection of the fox hole, the soldier waited for a chance to push the mine under the tracks of any Allied tank using the road. Another one-man attack method uses the lunge mine, which consists of an armor-piercing charge placed on the end of a pole. The attacker waits in hiding and lunges at the first tank to draw near with his mine and pole held in much the same manner as a rifle with fixed bayonet. The mine explodes on contact.

A demolition charge, manually attached to an Allied tank and hand-detonated, is another suicide weapon employed by the Japanese. Filled with 10½ pounds of picric acid, a wooden box about 8 to 10 inches square is mounted on a wooden base and slung over the back of the soldier. The outside perimeter of the box is fringed with hooks by which the tank raider hangs the demolition charge on the turret or any other part of the Allied tank. A Type 91 or 97 hand grenade is used as a detonator. After the box is attached to the tank, the fuze head of the grenade is rapped sharply by the tank hunter; an explosion results immediately.

Another weapon is the shoulder-pack mine. With the mine strapped to his back, the Japanese conceals himself as close as possible to the path of the approaching tank. When the tank arrives at a point about 15 feet from the concealed soldier, he dashes out and throws himself under it, between the tracks. He pulls a detonating cord when the tank is directly over him. The mine explodes 1 to 3 seconds after the cord is pulled.

In recent operations in Burma much reliance was placed on one-man suicide tank-hunting tactics. Types of suicide activities varied. Soldiers sat in fox holes with aerial bombs between their knees, pre-

Figure 208.—Type of improvised charge employed in suicide attack.

pared to detonate them by hand when an Allied tank passed over. Attempts were made to place picric acid charges with pull fuzes on tanks by hand. Hand grenades and Molotov cocktails were thrown from hiding places in culverts. Other Japanese were reported to have attempted to set tanks on fire by throwing lighted branches which had been dipped in oil. One Japanese officer charged a tank armed only with his sword and succeeded in inflicting considerable personal injuries on the tank crew.

A report from Okinawa told of Japanese soldiers hidden in camouflaged holes and armed with explosive charges strapped to their backs. Success of this antitank ruse required that the hidden soldiers detonate the charges, using pull igniters, as Allied tanks passed over the holes.

These tactics illustrate a recently discerned Japanese trend to resort more and more to the use of individual tank hunters rather than teams. This practice apparently follows a known decision of the Japanese Imperial General Staff that tank-assault units can be used most efficiently if each individual member of such units acts upon his own initiative in suicide attacks. Tactics are modified to provide supporting fire for individual attackers in order to enable them to get within striking distance of their targets.

Antitank Obstacles

If they have sufficient time the Japanese always construct antitank obstacles around a defensive position. These generally take the form of ditches and barricades, usually covered by antitank or small-arms fire. Like other armies, the Japanese use artificial and natural obstacles to impede or stop the movement of armored vehicles and bring them under the fire of covering weapons, or else to channelize the movement of tanks into areas where they can be attacked to advantage. Obstacles are often sited so that they supplement natural antitank barriers.

The improvised nature of Japanese obstacles is their outstanding characteristic. They are constructed largely of materials available locally, or are improvisations from weapons or material intended for other purposes. An example of this improvisation recently occurred in Burma where a so-called "fire belt" obstacle was laid down by dumping oil on a road, to be ignited as the tanks entered the oiled area. The Japs also used flaming obstacles in the recent fighting in Borneo.

It is common practice for the Japanese to use several different types of antitank obstacles in a single defensive position, but their general form and nature remain constant. Materials used for obstacle construction, as well as size and method of construction, vary

Figure 209.—Antitank ditch and antitank-gun emplacement covering ditch (Saipan).

Figure 210.—Antitank ditch on Saipan.

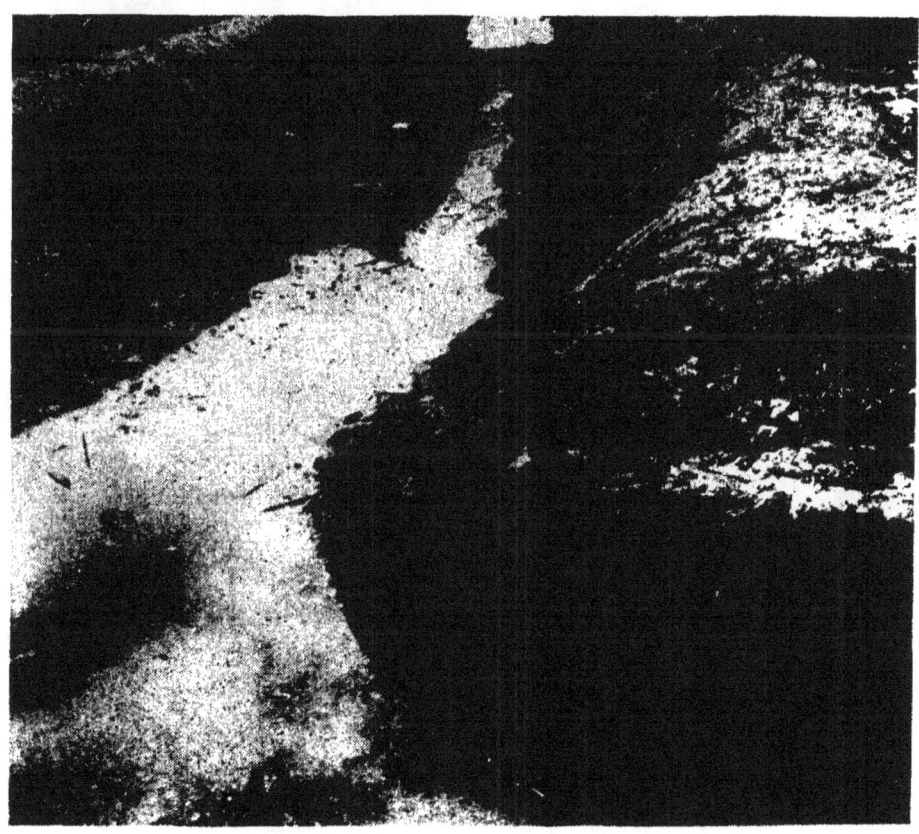

Figure 211.—Oil-filled antitank ditch in Borneo.

with the nature of the terrain and with the equipment of hostile forces. Any of the antitank obstacles can be used either as road blocks or as continuous barriers, in inland defense or as beach obstacles.

Ditches

The antitank ditch, one of the most common Japanese antitank obstacles, has been used on nearly all of the defended Pacific islands, both as a beach obstacle and as an inland tank barrier. It has also been used in Burma where one Japanese antitank ditch was reported to be over a mile long. In some places, ditches are divided at regular intervals into cells or sections by earth walls, a foot or two wide.

Ditches thus far encountered in the Pacific theater vary from 10 to 20 feet in width and from 5 to 10 feet in depth. The most common cross sections are triangular and trapezoidal. The soil is usually piled on the Japanese side of the ditch, thereby increasing its effective depth. The ditch may be camouflaged with palm fronds or other material, and sometimes the soil is removed or scattered to facilitate concealment. On occasion, tank ditches may be covered completely, thus constituting traps large enough to engulf an entire tank.

Log Barricades

The log barricade is a commonly used antitank obstacle. It has a number of variations. One of the simplest types, consisting of

Figure 212.—Log barricade on Makin Atoll.

horizontal logs attached to trees 3 to 4 feet above the ground, is used in woods or where heavy timber is available. A contrasting type consists of a solid wall of logs placed horizontally between vertical posts. A more common variation consist of two or three rows of horizontal logs attached to braced vertical posts. This barricade, about 5 feet high, consists of native timber logs at least 1 foot in diameter. This type of barricade is also used as a beach and as an underwater obstacle.

Posts

Post obstacles consist of a field, or series, of timber or concrete posts. Post obstacles are prescribed for use as both land and underwater obstacles. They may be made more effective by inclination in the direction from which the attack is expected.

Timber posts are most common, and the Japanese state that they should be oak and at least 12 inches in diameter. If palm logs are used, they must be braced. Palm-log posts have been strengthened by fastening three posts together in a clover leaf. The posts, from 5 to 10 feet long, are placed with an average of two-thirds of their length in the ground. Standard Japanese patterns call for one, two, or three rows.

Instructions for the construction and use of concrete-post obstacles have been issued by the Japanese, though there are no reports that such obstacles have been encountered in actual operations. Plans prescribe a post 6 to 7 feet long and about a foot square, with both vertical and horizontal steel reinforcing. Such posts are emplaced with about one-third of their length embedded in concrete bases in one, two, or three rows, with 5 to 7 feet between rows, and with the posts in each row 6 to 10 feet apart.

Abatis

The abatis is a simple but less effective obstacle. It consists of large trees felled with the tops toward the enemy so that the branches become intermingled. The Japanese make their widest use of this obstacle as a road block. Trees along a narrow road can be prepared for demolition and then blown at the last minute. The Japanese have employed this method in Burma. In a few cases, mines or booby traps have been placed in the abatis.

Walls

The Japanese have constructed very few solid concrete walls. But wall obstacles have been constructed of native rock held in place with cement or mortar. Such walls are at least 4 feet high and are generally back-filled. They are designed to be sufficiently high that a tank cannot climb over them, and strong enough to resist being overturned or destroyed by gunfire. A wall-type obstacle, found on some Pacific islands, was constructed of palm tree stumps. The excavated stumps were piled with roots pointed towards the avenues of approach for Allied tanks.

Antitank Obstacles in Cities

In the defense of Manila, the Japanese used as strongpoints all types of earthquake-proof structures such as private homes, churches, schools, and government buildings, and covered approaches to these

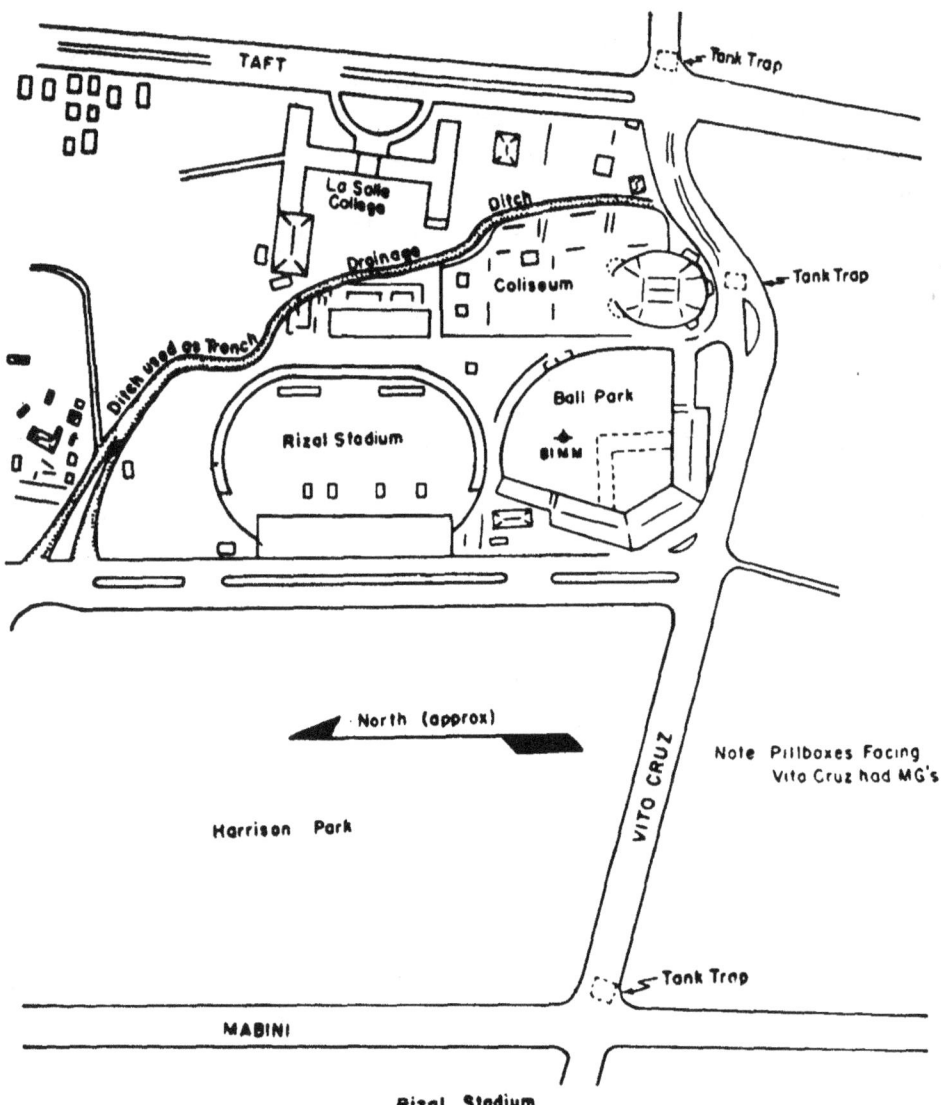

Figure 213.—Antitank obstacles in Manila.

buildings with antitank weapons sited in the buildings. The approaches to these strongpoints also were blocked by obstacles and mines and covered by antitank weapons, most of which were protected by heavily sandbagged pillboxes.

Full advantage was taken of existing stone walls around houses and buildings to add to the strength and completeness of the interconnected array of delaying obstacles. In one area, a drainage ditch 15 feet wide and 10 feet deep was used as a natural tank trap, and this approach was further protected by a concrete wall 15 feet high and 2 feet thick.

Streets were blocked by a variety of obstacles. Intersections were barricaded and defended with antitank weapons sited to cover the intersecting streets. Steel posts, imbedded in concrete, were used as street obstacles, and, in one instance, railroad-car axles were set upright in the pavement. In other cases, heavy factory machinery was moved into the city streets and there firmly embedded. One kind of antitank obstacle was constructed of fuel drums set upright and arranged in two or more columns. The space between these columns was then filled with earth, as were the drums themselves. Conventional antitank ditches were used in Manila, and existing shell craters were developed into antitank obstacles.

Minefields

The Japanese did not begin to use mines effectively until after the Saipan campaign. Prior to that time, minefields were generally poorly sited and camouflaged, and often appeared to have been laid merely to get them into the ground. In recent operations, however, minefields have been much more soundly employed. The Japanese have prescribed standard patterns and principles for the use of mines, but in actual practice they seldom apply their doctrine. In some instances, mines are laid between or near other antitank obstacles, in areas that are difficult to cover with fire power, or in terrain where construction of other obstacles is difficult.

Where Allied units are known to have armor, the laying of mines is considered to be the essential duty of the Japanese division engineer regiment. In one particular operation involving a division it is known that 12,000 mines were laid.

Common Minefield Sites

Mines are used on beaches in one or both of the following areas: that section of the beach lying between high tide and low tide levels, and the area from 25 to 30 yards inland. Usually the mines are laid in rows, with rows from a few feet to 10 yards apart; individual mines in a particular row may be spaced from 10 to 30 feet apart. In recent operations, however, the Japanese have neglected the mining of beaches in favor of inland defenses.

Mines are frequently found in large open fields, or in the area that may be termed the approaches to the field. Their employment in most cases is the same as that inland from the beach. They are placed in rows with no standard distance between rows.

Ordinarily, junctions of roads and approaches to bridges are mined. Special attention is given to mining the shoulders of the road in the vicinity of such areas.

The field of fire from a pillbox is necessarily limited. Therefore, land mines are sometimes used to cover the approaches bordering this

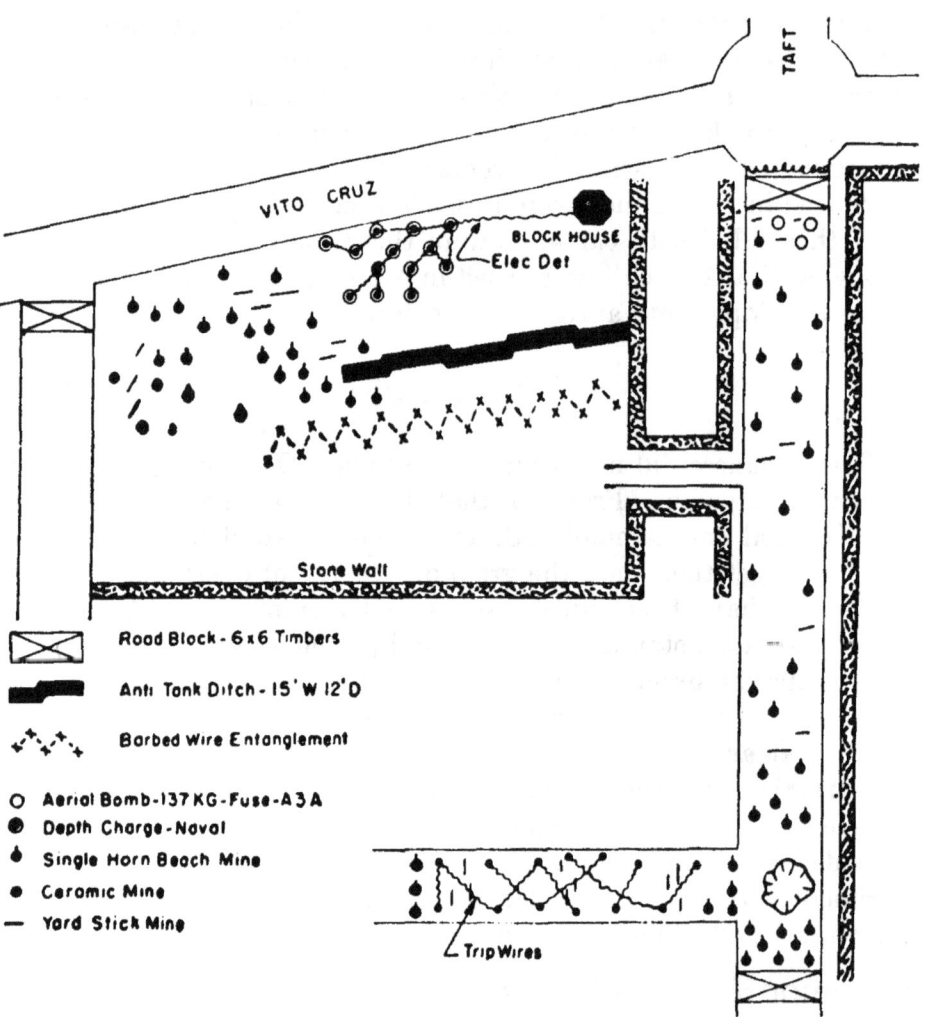

Figure 214.—Vito Cruz minefield in Manila.

comparatively narrow field of fire. Approaches to Japanese antitank barricades and detours around them are likely to be mined and covered with fire from neighboring positions, but this is not a consistent practice.

Mines in Manila

In the battle for Manila, the Japanese made extensive use of mines. Controlled and uncontrolled minefields, as well as combinations of both types, were found on roads, at street intersections, on bridges and their approaches, in the vicinity of barricades, and in open lots. Most minefields were covered by fire. No regular pattern of minefield construction was noted; mines were likely to be encountered anywhere. In general, they were poorly camouflaged, with many mines only partially buried and quite easy to locate.

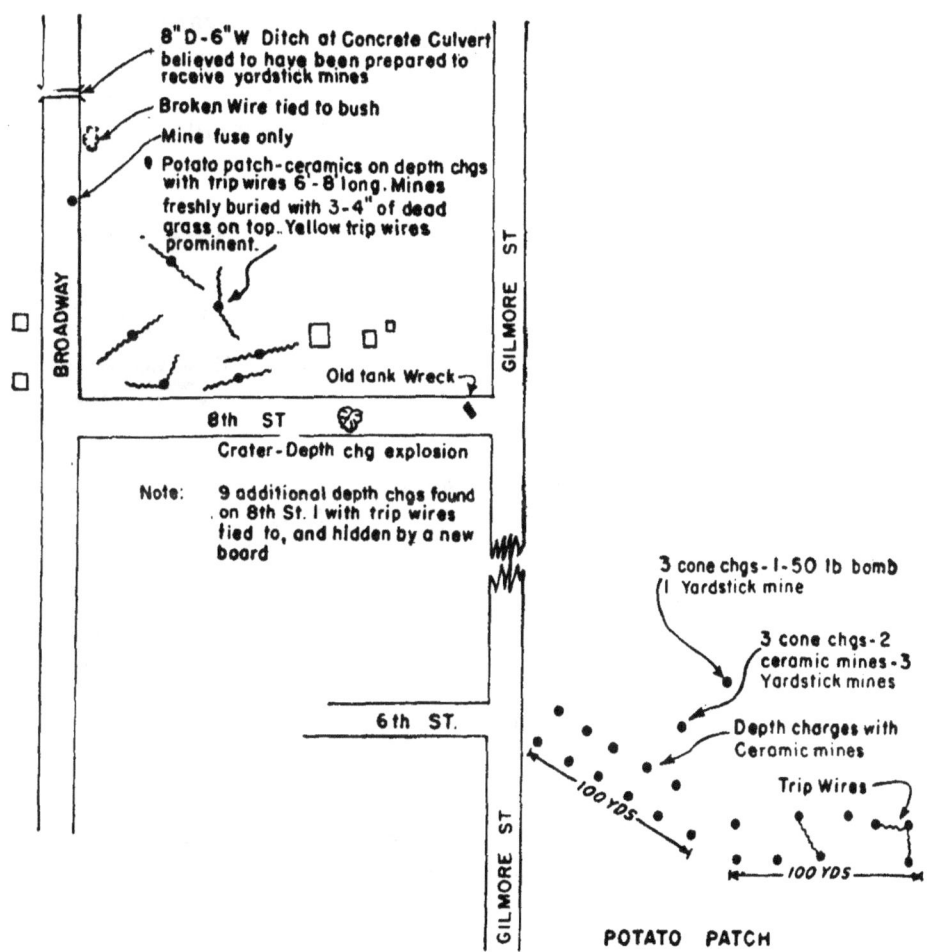

Figure 215.—Typical minefield in Manila.

All types of mines and explosives were used and indiscriminately mixed. Antiboat mines were most common, with aerial bombs converted to land-mine use next most frequently employed. These two types were frequently found together, in the proportion of two antiboat mines to one aerial bomb. In addition, artillery shells, mortar shells, and depth charges were often used as mines. Depth charges ordinarily were prepared for electrical detonation, with control wires leading to concealed positions. Depth charges were also placed on end 6 to 8 inches below ground level. On the top of the depth charge was a Type 3 pottery or Type 93 yardstick mine flush with the ground. In fields and on grassy road shoulders, depth charges were encountered, with pottery mine detonators and trip wires, either single or interconnected. Fifty-five gallon drums contained depth charges with pottery mines attached. This combination was most often used in road blocks.

Pottery mines were frequently trip-wired, and yardstick mines were scattered on road surfaces or placed above buried 100-pound aerial bombs. In other instances, aerial bombs were found set with a nose-impact fuze close to the surface of the ground; a 50-pound pressure was sufficient to cause detonation.

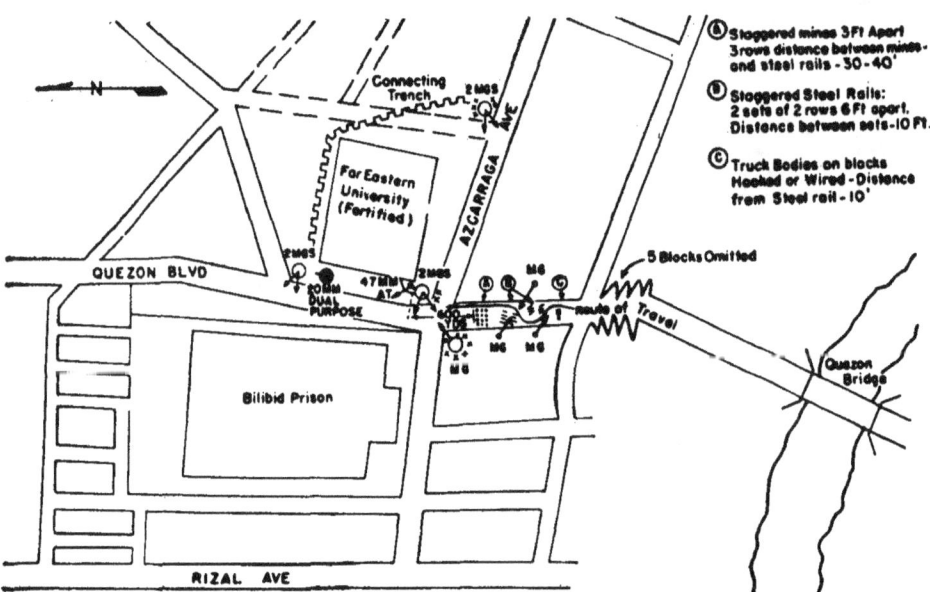

Figure 216.—Minefields and obstacles with covering weapons in the Far Eastern University area in Manila.

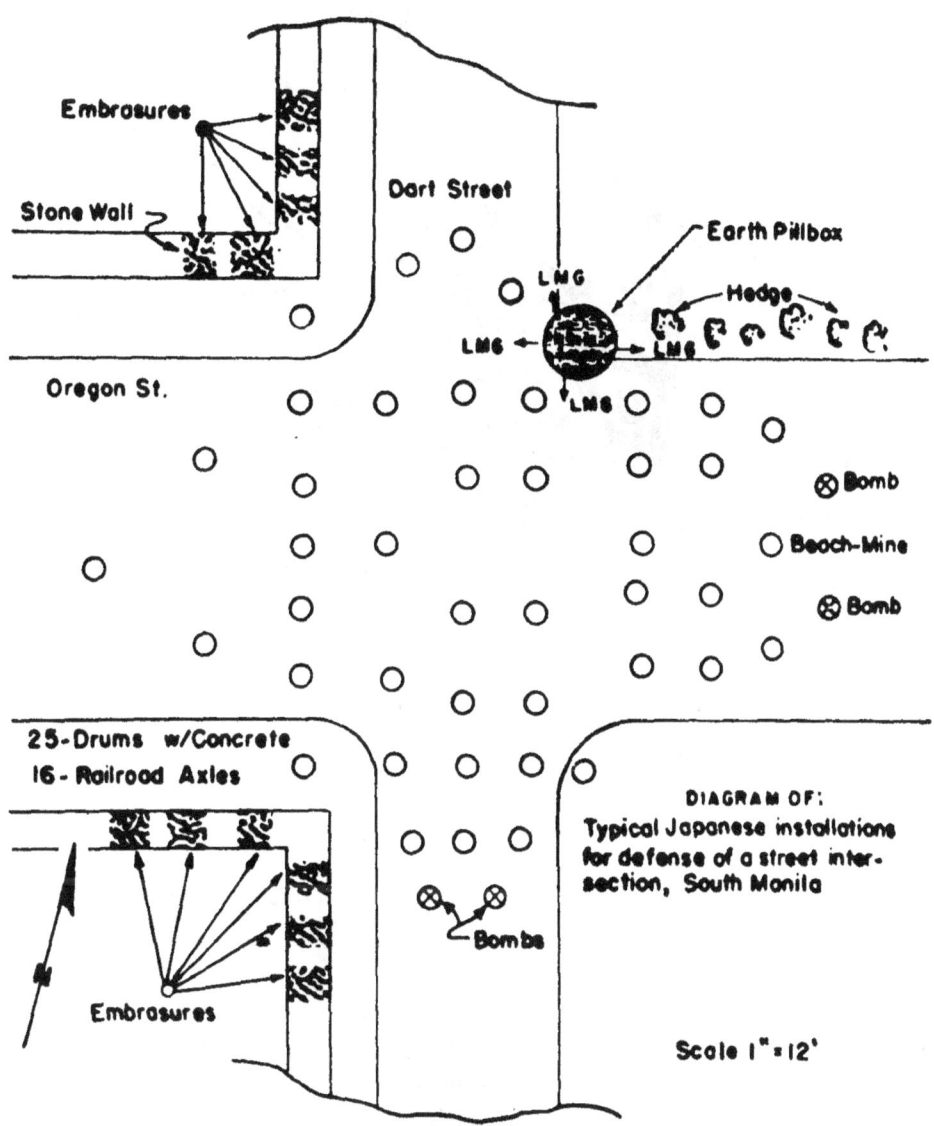

Figure 217.—Typical Japanese installation for the defense of a street intersection in south Manila.

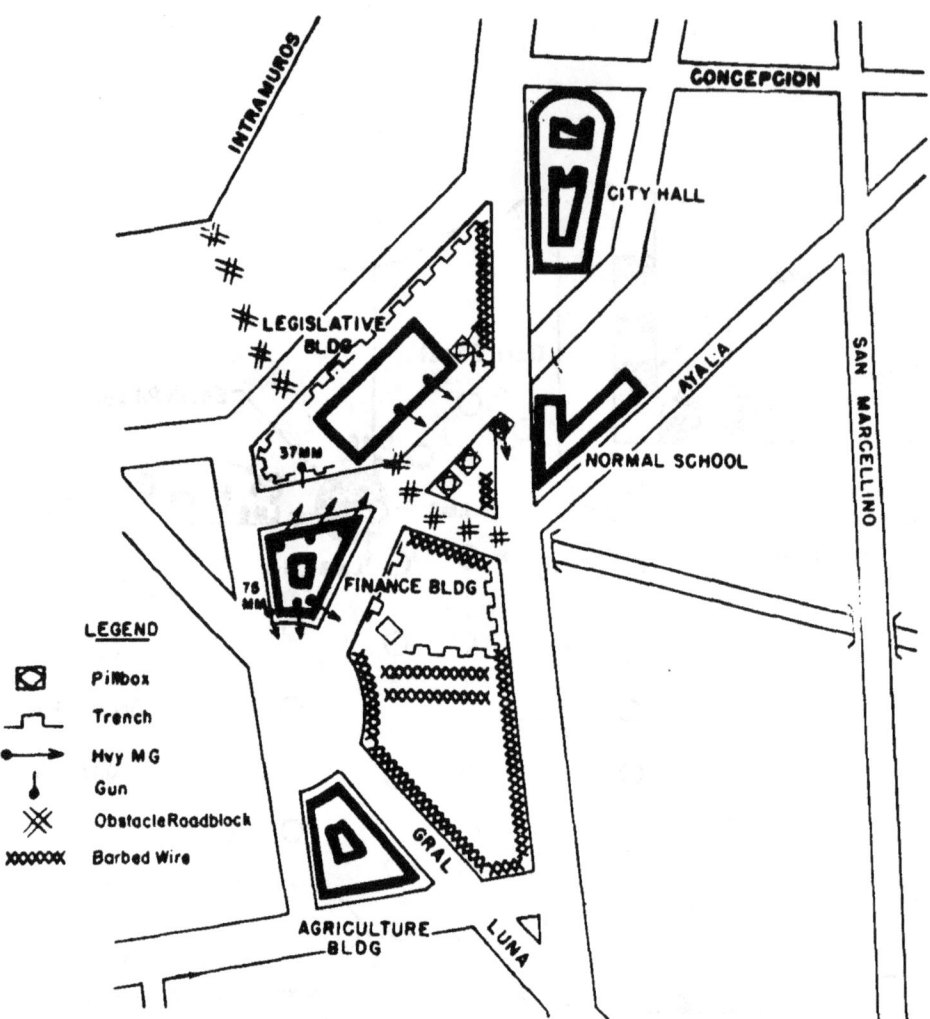

Figure 218.—Organization of streets and buildings in Manila.

Methods of Laying Mines

The Japanese either lay mines on top of the ground or bury them so that the fuzes are at ground level or ½ inch below. The Type 93 tape-measure mine, often used in antitank minefields, does not always damage the track of a medium tank sufficiently to disable it. The Japanese therefore generally lay tape-measure mines on top of one another, in pairs or in tiers of three or four, or place booster charges under single mines.

In most fighting areas there has been a total lack of uniformity in Japanese minefield patterns, even in minefields laid by troops in the same command. In fact, many fields have had no pattern, and

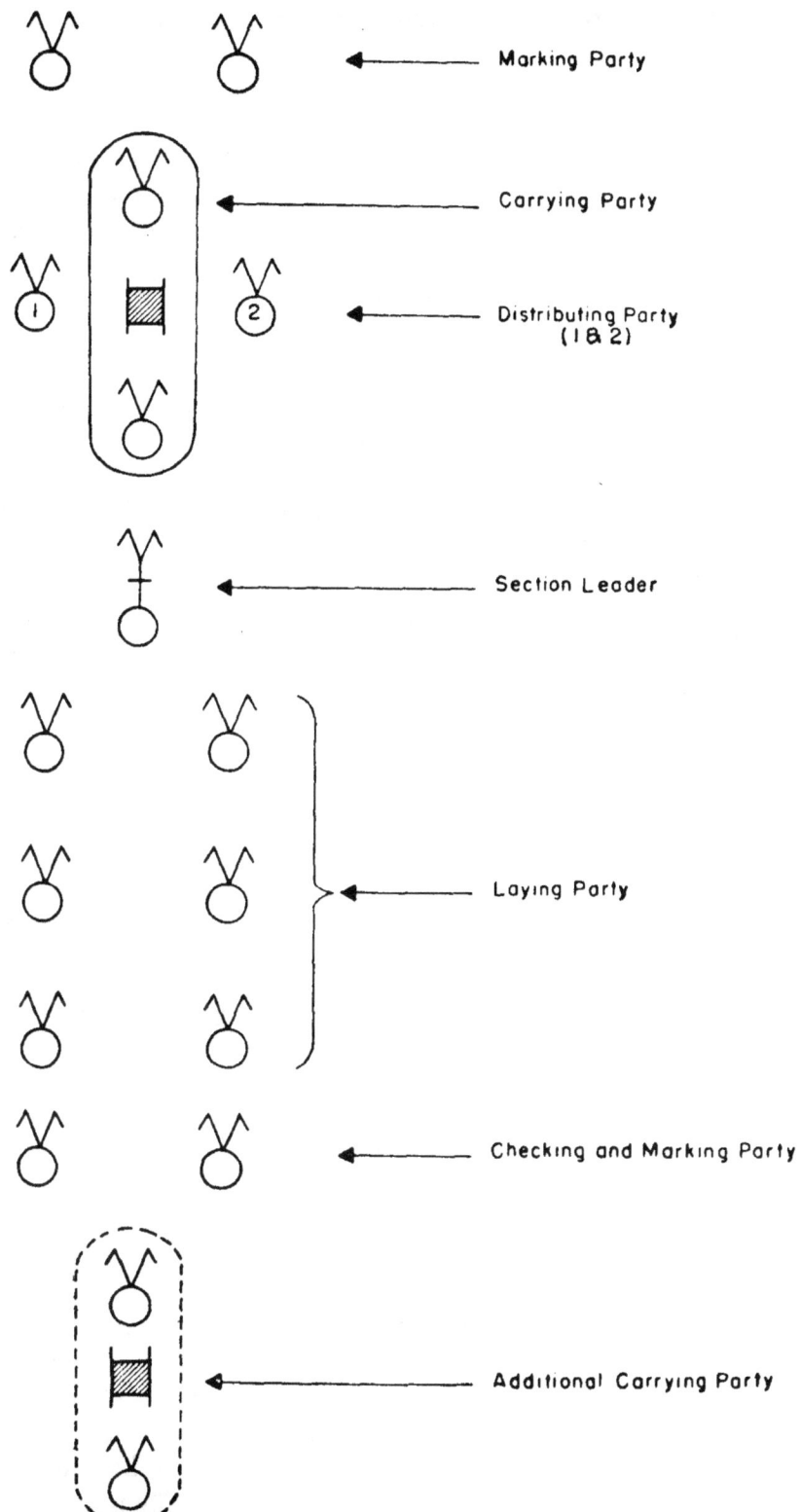

Figure 219.—Organization and duties of Japanese mine-laying section, diagram.

207

apparently were placed by troops ignorant of antitank minefield doctrine.

The Japanese have made an occasional use of dummy minefields. Some have been constructed of branches or bricks and then covered with earth. Aerial bombs have been placed uncovered and unfuzed along roadways. These dummy minefields, intentionally obvious, are designed to slow down tank attacks and minesweeping efforts, or to force tanks off the road and over fox holes occupied by suicide parties.

When sufficient time is available for previous preparation, the Japanese dig holes for minefields to be located in an area covering the anticipated advance of Allied armor. Mines are distributed to several points forward of the area to be mined and are buried at the time of the expected attack by hostile tanks. If terrain restricts and channelizes the movement and advance of Allied armor, Japanese mines are often laid beforehand. When this is done, particular attention is paid to moisture-proofing the mines. Mines that are not completely moisture-proof are kept well-covered until emplaced.

When under fire, and pressed for time, the Japanese may organize a mine-laying section with assigned responsibilities as illustrated in Figure 220.

Designation	Personnel	Mission Task	Equipment
Section Leader		General supervision	One-meter ruler.
Marking Party	2	Marking positions; assisting in laying	Two marking ropes; one shovel or one pick each.
Distributing Party	2	Distributing mines; assisting in laying	One shovel or one pick each.
Carrying Party	4–6	Carrying of mines	Two to three litters for carrying mines.
Laying Party	6	Laying of mines	One shovel or one pick each.
Checking and Marking Party	2	Marking; checking	Two shovels each; marking materials.

Figure 220.—Organization and duties of Japanese mine-laying section.

The section leader indicates the forward boundary of the field, density of mines, the number of rows and the method of laying and marking. He also prescribes the time limits for completion of the task. The marking party ties down one end of the marking rope, extending the other end in the direction indicated by the section leader. This operation is repeated for each row. The marking rope,

Designation	Personnel	Mission		Equipment
Section Leader		General supervision		1 set liaison equipment. 1 land mine.
Hasty Laying Party Group 1	5	Lay mines		1 Type 3 land mine, 1 Type 93 land mine (2 together). 5 stick mines, improvised mines (2-kg explosive) etc. per man.
Hasty Laying Party Group 2.	5			1 shovel or pick, improvised small shovel, mine-carrying equipment per man.
Close-Assault Party	4	1.	Watch for opportunity to attack	1 hollow-charge rifle-grenade launcher. 1 frangible incendiary grenade. 1 frangible smoke grenade.
		2.	Immobilize tank	2 stick mines. 2 hand grenades.
		3.	Same as above	2 Type 3 hand-thrown mines. 2 antipersonnel mines.
		4.	Boarding attack	2 Type 3 hand-thrown mines. 2 hand grenades. 1 Pick.
Supporting Party	3	1.	Attack tank-borne infantry	1 light machine gun. 2 hand grenades.
		2.	Same as above	LMG ammunition. 2 hand grenades.
		3.	Attack or hinder enemy tank	1 hollow-charge rifle-grenade launcher. 1 grenade launcher. 1 self-propelled smoke candle.

Remarks: 1. Hasty laying of mines should be done in two rows 50 yards wide, at intervals of 2 yards.
2. The section is composed of 11 engineers and an infantry squad of seven men. The infantry squad leader is responsible for close assault and support.
3. The small improvised shovel is made of bamboo, or other material. It is used for laying mines.

Figure 221.—Composition of hasty minefield-laying section.

about 20 yards long, is divided into intervals to indicate the proper spacing of mines. Either end of the marking rope can be fastened to the ground.

The carrying party, at the beginning of the operation, follows the marking party and delivers mines to the distributing party. The distributing party, following on each side of the carrying party, distributes the mines to the marked points. The laying party, divided into two groups, buries the mines in each row. The checking and marking party then inspects the work of the laying party and marks the minefield. A mine-laying section as illustrated in Figure 220 can lay a minefield composed of Type 3 pottery land mines at the rate of 100 yards in 10 to 15 minutes.

Figure 221 illustrates the composition, duties, and equipment of a mine section organized to operate under close-combat conditions in hasty laying of mines.

The section leader assigns the assault and support parties their missions, and for purposes of coordination usually takes command of the hasty mine-laying group. The section leader indicates the general plan, the group's limits of responsibility, and action to be taken after the laying task is completed.

Mine-laying group leaders issue mines to each individual in the group. Leaders then instruct individuals on the interval to be taken by each man, location of markers, and, when necessary, action to be taken subsequent to laying the mines. Guided by the movement of skirmishers, each man is stationed at a pre-designated point. Particular attention is paid to fixing the intervals between men. If two rows of mines are to be laid, the one nearer the approaching tanks is laid first. Whether mines are buried or merely laid on the ground depends upon the immediate situation.

Throughout the operation it is considered essential that close contact be kept with supporting units. Occasionally smoke will be used after completion of the minefield to conceal the location and extent of the mined area.

In night mine-laying operations, the carriers who lay the mines may work in pairs, or in teams of one carrier and one layer.

Methods of Marking Minefields

Many Japanese believe that their language is undecipherable to Allied troops, and as a result do not hesitate to mark openly danger spots such as areas and installations that have been mined. In one minefield, in New Guinea, over 20 signs, written in Japanese, were used to define the mined areas. Principal warning signs likely to be

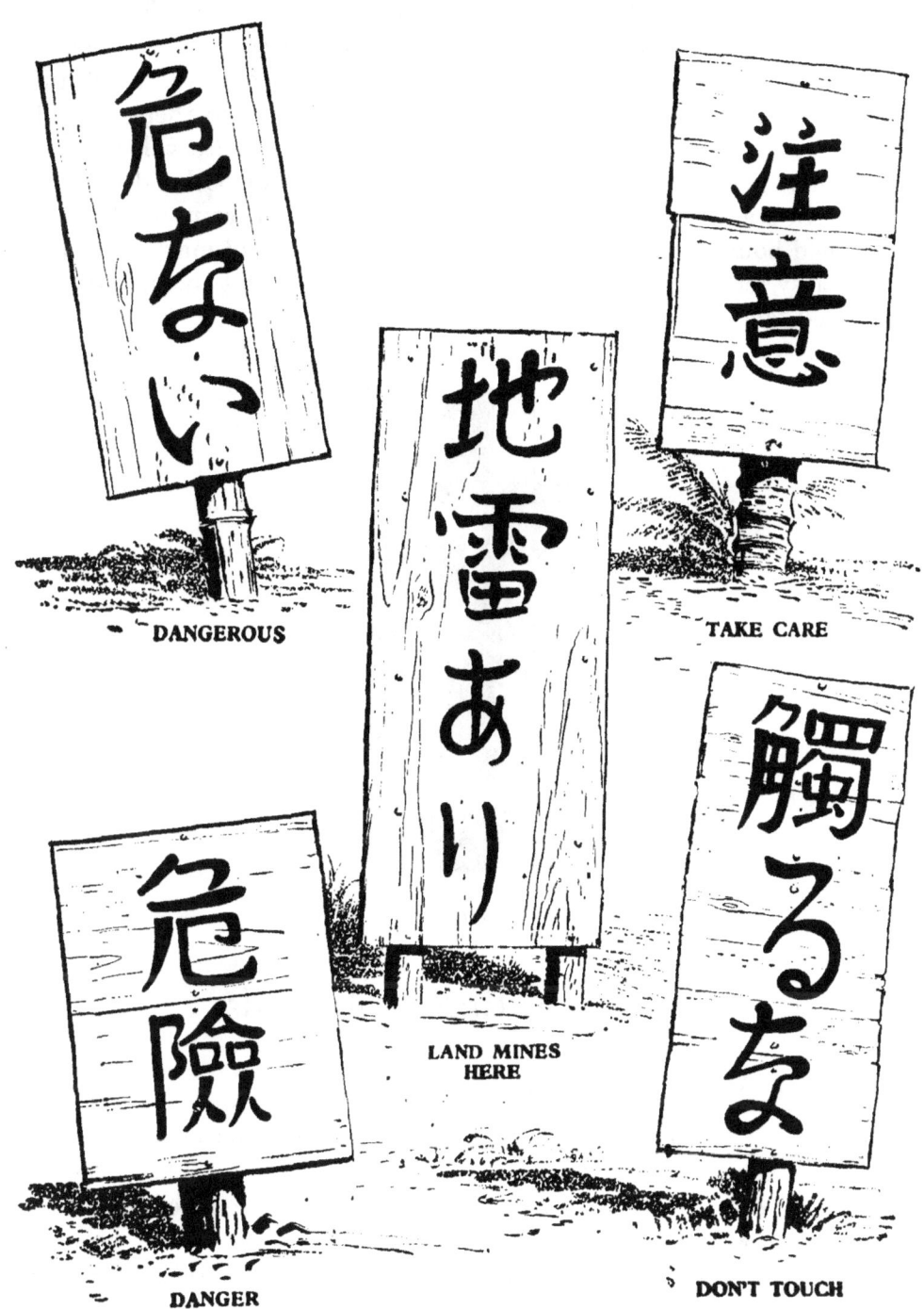

Figure 222.—Japanese minefield warning signs.

encountered by Allied troops in the field are illustrated in Figure 222.

Japanese Regulations on Antitank Combat prescribe that minefield markers generally are to be placed to indicate not only the front and rear boundaries of the minefield but safe lanes through them as well. These boundaries are designated by stakes placed at intervals of 10 to 20 yards. Safe lanes of travel are marked on one or both sides of the lane with stakes set at the same space interval as that prescribed for minefield boundaries. Figure 223 illustrates a type of marker used in low grassy terrain. It is made of bamboo, and the flat cut-out surface is placed facing friendly troops.

Figure 223.—Japanese minefield marker.

Recent Antitank Methods

Antitank Methods in the Philippines

The Japanese used their normal antitank methods in the Philippines, with special emphasis on suicide tank-hunting parties. These suicide parties were used extensively, but although they accounted for a few tanks, they were largely unsuccessful. Some of these attack groups, after entering the Allied perimeter, lost their nerve or became so excited that they threw their explosive charges indiscriminately and inflicted little damage.

Comparatively few minefields were encountered in the Philippines, and, since the Japanese used little skill in camouflaging individual mines, the few fields that were encountered were easily detected.

Nevertheless the Japanese showed considerable skill in their use of single mines, especially in night infiltration attacks. On these night raids, they placed the mine or other explosives on or within the tank, detonated the charge, and attempted a getaway. Often no effort was made to detonate the mine; instead, it was placed under a tank truck or along a much-used road, and on the following morning the first movement of the tank detonated the charge.

Little that was unique was observed in the Japanese use of antitank guns in the Philippines. In general, when guns were employed in tank terrain, the Japanese chose positions which afforded excellent fields of fire, dug in the individual guns, and provided adequate small-arms protection.

Antitank Methods on Okinawa

Combat instructions issued by the Japanese prior to the Allied invasion of Okinawa reveal that the defensive organization of their positions was based on the proposition that "Allied combat strength lies in their tanks." Plans for defense against these tanks included complete preparations for blocking vital routes by the fire of all types of weapons, by the use of mines, and by the construction of some antitank obstacles. Japanese appreciation of terrain was excellent, and much attention was given to limiting and channelizing the maneuverability of Allied armor by the coordinated use of all antitank measures. Fire from commanding terrain by antitank weapons, field artillery, antiaircraft artillery employed in a ground role, and mortars was relied upon to a greater extent than antitank obstacles. Many unimportant roads were cut by demolitions. Antitank ditches were well camouflaged, and the tendency was to prepare them as pitfall traps rather than as conventional ditches. Bridges were blown consistently and trees were felled across roads as hasty delaying obstacles.

To extend and supplement these more conventional methods, suicide and assault-team tank-hunters were organized. The Japanese paid special attention to coordinating these operations with supporting fire of all arms. Foot troops or tankborne infantry supporting Allied armor were the particular targets for Japanese fire from automatic weapons, mortars, grenade dischargers, and battalion guns. Fifteen seconds after fire from these weapons ceased, Japanese combat instructions called for close-in assault against the Allied tanks, and in some instances this close coordination was achieved.

In some close-quarter attacks, a Japanese soldier armed with satchel charges, bangalore torpedoes, pole charges, and antitank mines ran alongside an Allied tank and endeavored to stay with the vehicle until he could destroy it by a suicidal attack. It should be emphasized that the death of the individual was accepted as the necessary price for the destruction of the tank, in accordance with the Japanese doctrine of "one soldier, one tank." Japanese close-quarter tank attacks are not designed solely for the purpose of committing honorable suicide; the attack is expected to achieve definite military results. Tanks that were halted during the fighting in towns and cities by natural or artificial obstacles and by gunfire were subject to these tank-hunter operations.

In one Japanese infantry division, small, picked raiding parties, called mortar- and tank-destruction units, were ordered to infiltrate Allied lines and cause as much destruction as possible to Allied armor and mortars.

In addition to Types 91, 97, and 99 hand grenades, the Japanese on Okinawa used the Type 3 conical hand-thrown mine. This mine appears to have been an item of general issue to small units. Many of these mines were found without the stabilizing hemp or straw tail which ensures that the mine will hit the tank in the correct position for the maximum explosive effect. This is a possible indication that the Japanese were instructed to place the charge directly against the tank rather than risk failure of the thrown mine to make proper contact. Large quantities of stick-type fragmentation and stick-type incendiary grenades were also employed.

The use of land mines on Okinawa was far better than in previous campaigns. Roads, particularly in the vicinity of bridges, were mined. All logical terrain approaches to defensive installations, and areas adjacent to and in the vicinity of caves, also were effectively mined. Reports indicate that at least one electrically controlled minefield was installed on the island. Definite minefield patterns were used in the vicinity of airfields, but irregular scattering of mines seemed most common. Mines often were camouflaged by indigenous vegetation. One field was laid in a cabbage patch, with heads of cabbage used as camouflage. The presence of the mines, however, was soon revealed by the wilting of the cut cabbage. One minefield was found to be composed entirely of single-horn antiboat mines, while in another locality 500-pound aerial bombs were used as makeshift land mines.

All types of light and heavy artillery and mortars were used effectively on Okinawa against Allied light and medium tanks. Fire from antitank weapons was often delivered at ranges as close as 50 yards. Most antitank fire, however, came from much greater distances. Antitank guns, sited in caves, acted as covering weapons to the approaches to the caves. Guns were sited so as to be in mutual support of each other. Antitank artillery was often sited to deliver flanking and, in some instances, rear fire on approaching tanks.

Some use of wire was reported on Okinawa. Inverted double-apron obstacles were the most common. Roll-wire obstacles were also used, as well as single- and double-strand wire.

For the most part, Japanese armor was used as dug-in pillboxes. Tanks were encountered well dug-in and sited as additional antitank defense. One coordinated infantry-tank dawn attack was reported. From the standpoint of the defender, the terrain and existing weather conditions limited the employment of tanks in their conventional role.

○

www.ingramcontent.com/pod-product-compliance
Lightning Source LLC
Chambersburg PA
CBHW081835170426
43199CB00017B/2732